T0010345

Joan Wulff's Fly Fishing

Expert Advice from a Woman's Perspective

Joan Salvato Wulff

STACKPOLE
BOOKS
Essex, Connecticut
Blue Ridge Summit, Pennsylvania

STACKPOLE BOOKS

An imprint of Globe Pequot, the trade division of
The Rowman & Littlefield Publishing Group, Inc.
4501 Forbes Blvd., Ste. 200
Lanham, MD 20706
www.rowman.com

Distributed by NATIONAL BOOK NETWORK

Illustrations on pages 30–37 and 150 by Francis W. Davis
Reach cast illustration on page 64 by Richard Harrington
All other illustrations by Michelflyn

British Library Cataloguing in Publication Information available

**The Library of Congress has cataloged the hardcover edition of this book as
follows:**

Wulff, Joan.
   [Fly fishing]
   Joan Wulff's fly fishing : expert advice from a woman's perspective. –
1st ed.
     p.   cm.
   1. Fly fishing. 2. Women fishers. I. Title. II. Title: Fly fishing.
SH456.W83   1991
799. 1'2–dc20

                                               91-12637
                                                CIP

ISBN 9780811775656 (paperback)
ISBN 9780811776455 (epub)

To the outdoor women with whom I share
a love of fly fishing
and
to the others who will one day
discover its joys.

Acknowledgments

I am indebted to John McDonald for his sage advice and for having made Dame Juliana Berners and the *Treatise on Fishing with an Angle* accessible in his book *The Origins of Angling*.

My thanks to:

Frank and Mary Visconti for the cottage at Lake Mystic where this was begun.

Don Johnson, director, and Joe Pisarro, research/publicity volunteer, at the American Museum of Fly Fishing at Manchester, Vermont, for providing the following material: "The Girls of Summer," by Ken Cameron, *The Flyfisher*: Part 1, Volume 5, #3, Summer 1977, and Part 2, Volume 5, #4, Fall 1977; "Carrie G. Stevens and the Woman Fly Fisher's Club" by Susie Isaksen, *The American Fly Fisher*, Volume 3, #4, Fall 1976 and Volume 8, #4, Fall 1981; "Cornelia 'Fly Rod' Crosby," by Austin Hogan, *The American Fly Fisher*, Volume 4, #4, Fall 1977; and information from *American Fly Fishing: A History*, by Paul Shullery.

Rick Hafele and Scott Roederer for help from their book *An Angler's Guide to Aquatic Insects and Their Imitations*.

Dianne Russell, for instigating this project.

Biologist Tony Bonavist, Ed Van Put, and all the anglers and writers from whose experience I have benefited.

And to my best friend, Lee Wulff, with whom I have shared the excitement of fly fishing for the past twenty-four years, for his wisdom, inspiration, and encouragement.

Contents

Preface to the 2024 Edition

When I entered the sport of fly fishing for trout—in the 1930s—it was a man's sport, pure and simple: rods were heavy, constructed of bamboo; waders were made of canvas and rubber—death traps to me—so women were limited to boys' hip boots.

Rod materials lightened up over the years, but men were not encouraging wives or girlfriends to join them. It was still a man's sport! I think I was one of two or three women trying to make a living in the fishing world in the 1950s, '60s, and '70s.

In 1979, my husband, Lee Wulff, and I started a fly fishing school in the Catskills of New York. It still took three years before the first woman came to the school on her own.

To make a long story short, it was Robert Redford's film *A River Runs Through It*, in 1992, that changed everything and brought women into the sport in huge numbers. They saw the beautiful rivers on which we fish—and the handsome men I used to have all to myself!

As a result, we had more women than men in our school for twelve years! Now it is split 50/50.

Having waited most of my life for all of this to happen, I can now die happy!

Enjoy!

Introduction

As is true of many of the women of my generation who fly fish, my father was a fly fisherman. Mother was not. It became apparent the first time I accompanied them for an evening of fly fishing for bass that Dad had all the fun while Mom got yelled at for not keeping the rowboat at the right distance from bass cover. Unencumbered by the knowledge that women didn't fish, it was obvious to me then, at age five or six, that it was better to be the fisherman than the rower.

My dad, Jimmy Salvato, gave up an accounting job in his mid-twenties to become the proprietor of the Paterson Rod and Gun Store. Despite a seventy-hour work week, he wrote an outdoor column for the *Paterson Morning Call*, helped to start most of the conservation clubs in northern New Jersey, hunted moose and woodcock, raised hunting dogs, and managed to fit in some tournament casting on summer Sundays.

The Paterson Casting Club met at the Oldham Pond near our home in North Haledon, and when the older of my two brothers, Jimmy, reached the age of eight, he went along with Dad to the club's practice sessions. Joan, who was ten, was bypassed.

I *wanted* to fly cast. Gaining Mom's permission to try it with Dad's fly rod one afternoon, I went to the casting club dock, put the rod together and flailed away. *Oops!* The tip and butt sections separated and, with no fly on the leader to stop it, the tip went into the six-foot-deep pond water. Home I went, crying and afraid of my father's anger. Mom may have been, too, because when our next-door neighbor came home from work, an hour before Dad would come in for dinner, she asked for his help. We went back to the dock with a garden rake and, bless Mr. Kuehn, he snagged it in a few minutes.

The Dad I didn't know very well, the authoritarian figure in my life, the man of whom I was a little bit afraid, asked me to join him and Jimmy the next Sunday at the casting club.

I can look back now and say I was born to fly cast. While it wasn't easy, I was drawn to it. That same year (1937) a friend, Eleanor Egg, had talked my parents into letting me take tap, ballet, and acrobatic lessons from her. I am convinced that the dancing lessons improved my casting because they taught me to use my whole body to back up my limited ten-year-old strength.

Casting and dancing became my favorite pastimes. I won my first casting title in 1938, the New Jersey Sub-Junior All Around Championship, and with it gained the motivation to practice. Although I took college preparatory courses in high school, when my guidance counsellor asked what my plans were ("I don't know") and what I liked to do ("fly cast and dance"), she suggested secretarial school.

I had started to teach tap dancing when I was thirteen and by the time I took my first job as a junior secretary with N.W. Ayer & Sons, an advertising agency in New York City, for $25 per week, I was earning $20 for teaching dancing on Saturdays. Just before I turned eighteen I gave up secretarial work for dancing and opened a school with Eleanor. How lucky I was! She instilled in me the joy of living, and of teaching, and we had a perfect partnership for eight years. I taught dancing for ten months of the year and competed as an amateur in five or six casting tournaments during the two summer months.

Between 1943 and 1951 I won one or more national women's titles every year and, in 1951, garnered four plus a fisherman's distance fly event against all-male competition. I beat the second-place winner—my boyfriend, Johnny Dieckman—by an average of one-third of a foot! This was an event in which I could master the tackle as well as the men because it was limited to what we now call a 9-weight line.

Distance fly casting had become my real love in tournaments. There were two distance fly events, the one mentioned above, with tackle suitable for actual fishing, and a second, the "unrestricted"

Joan at eighteen fly casting for *American Magazine*.

trout fly event, with specialty tackle capable of making casts so long as to be impractical for a fisherman. The event, which is still included in casting competitions, challenges casters to design tackle and develop techniques to cast a fly as far as is humanly possible with a one-handed rod. Interestingly, the average fly angler does benefit. The shooting-head line and the double-haul casting technique were either developed or refined through tournaments.

I had begun by "ghillying" for my casting mentor, William Taylor. After each cast I pulled the dozens of yards of shooting line back in from the water and spread them out on the dock beside him. I came to appreciate that distance fly casting was a sport of beautiful form and motion, requiring the use of the whole body. In 1947 I could no longer resist trying it, but I found Bill's tackle too heavy and so he made a lighter rod for me. Lighter? It weighed 6¾ ounces! (We had only bamboo to use then.)

For this event the silk line was specially constructed, by hand, of spliced sections of line of different diameters to form a taper. This tapered "head" was approximately fifty-two feet long and had a weight limitation of 1½ ounces. It was backed by monofilament shooting line and the record casts were 150 feet and up. I could not cast a line that heavy, so, once again, Bill Taylor made me a "lighter" one. It weighed 1⅜ ounces.

Even at those weights I could not false cast the outfit. I didn't have the strength to maintain line speed on a false cast, so all of my distance casting was done by taking the line off the water (with the head out of the rod tip), shooting on the backcast, and shooting the rest on the forward cast. In spite of my lack of strength, my coordination and timing allowed me to place about halfway down the line among the male competitors in most tournaments.

The longest cast I ever made in a national tournament was 144 feet, but in a registered New Jersey state tournament in 1960 I cast my fly 161 feet for an unofficial women's record. Unofficial because there weren't any, or enough, other women distance casters to have an event of our own. The men's record was less than 190 feet. Oh, that I could do it all again with graphite!

In 1948 fly casting brought me to the attention of angler, author, and famous hotelier Charles Ritz at a sportsmen's show in New York. Charles invited me to compete in the French National Tournament in Paris and in the International Casting Tournament in London, the first events of their kind to be held after the war. I won the International ⅝-ounce plug-casting championship, competing against men and women, professionals and amateurs.

Our dancing school, meanwhile, had become very successful. In 1952 I decided to leave, with Eleanor's blessing, after realizing that if I didn't make a conscious break, I might be there for the rest of my life. That would mean I would always miss spring trout fishing because of preparations for our June dance recital.

Making a living in the sport-fishing field was next to impossible in those days, but sportsmen's show exhibitions were available to me and the Ashaway Line & Twine Company hired me to do part-time goodwill work, calling on their dealers. In 1954 I did a series of shows in the Midwest with Monte Blue, star of the silent screen, as emcee. When I showed up in my shorts, hip boots, and creel, which was everyone's idea of a girl fisherman's costume, Monte took me aside and told me he wanted to try something different. "Wear a dress," he said, "a long one, and we'll wow 'em." Leaping at the chance to portray casting as feminine, I bought a strapless, ankle-length white dress with silver leaves on it, high-heeled sandals, and, to complete the outfit, rhinestones for my hair.

The combination was perfect and Monte presented my act beautifully, speaking softly while I was casting of grace, timing, and beauty. I didn't cast at targets but, instead, used one rod and then two, creating as many interesting patterns with the fly lines as I could in time with music. *Up a Lazy River* was a natural, and the audiences responded. It couldn't last forever, though, and without either Monte or an orchestra the costume didn't play as well mixed in with lumberjacks, retrievers, and Sparky the seal. I changed back to the shorts, boots, and creel outfit—but I'll remember the gown and music as being the perfect way to depict fly casting as an art form, especially suitable for women.

So there I was, a young woman in a man's field, gaining notoriety because of it, and feeling I was where I wanted to be. I had lots to learn; my fishing experience was broad but shallow. My generation of young women did not venture alone into the woods or streams. There were also the difficulties of the costume for stream fishing, and the discomforts of biting insects and bad weather. The gear, in a man's size small, was uncomfortable and "bug dope," as it was called, was greasy and strong smelling. Because I loved being outdoors, I thought of it as paying the price to get the rewards, but I did not fish as often or as comfortably as a young man my age might have done. There have been remarkable advances in the area of comfort, for both men and women, in the last fifteen years.

In 1959, married and with one child, I took a part-time job with the Garcia Corporation, which was, then, the largest tackle company in the world. I lived in Florida at the time but my job was to promote their products, through clinics and exhibitions, anywhere in the country. Part of the job was to fish in tournaments and that was a real bonus. Just like any other woman, juggling a career and a family left me little time for recreational fishing.

Years later, as part of my work, I had the opportunity to appear in a film on giant bluefin-tuna fishing that Lee Wulff was producing for ABC's *American Sportsman* television series. Although Lee and I knew each other casually, it was our first opportunity to fish together. After our marriage in 1967, my fishing horizons expanded. We traveled to the West for trout, the Canadian Maritime Provinces and Iceland for Atlantic salmon, and to Ecuador for marlin. We became a team for Garcia and held fly-fishing clinics and programs for clubs throughout the country.

My presence attracted women to these events. In earlier generations, men had gone on fishing trips partly to "get away from the wife," but now fishermen asked me to direct my words to their wives or girlfriends, hoping to convert them into companions who could share the pleasure of fly fishing. In 1979 Lee and I opened a fly-fishing school in New York's Catskill Mountains. Soon one-quarter of our students were women, and that percentage has now risen to one-third.

It is estimated that there are two million committed fly fishermen in the United States. Only 10 percent of those, two hundred thousand or less, subscribe to the fly-fishing magazines, and readership is reported as 96 percent male. If as many as 50 or 60 percent of those male readers shares life with a woman, there is a great potential to swell our ranks. The greater the number of fly fisherwomen, the more likely it is that the manufacturers of equipment and clothing will cater to our special needs.

It has taken all of my life for the changes to develop in equipment and attitude that now make fly fishing a natural extension of a woman's love of the outdoors. Whether you are married to a fisherman or are a single woman, there is nothing to stop you now except lack of time. Fortunately, one of the strengths of our sex is our high tolerance for interruption.

When Stackpole Books asked me to write this book, my first thought was, "Why do women need a book written especially for them when everything anyone needs to know about fly fishing has already been written?" It was necessary for me to answer my own question and as I did, the project became a journey of discovery. We have a heritage, from an admittedly small number of women, of which we can be very proud. There are already a few clubs in the United States whose membership is comprised solely of women who fly fish, and new clubs are springing up as I write. Our numbers are growing to the extent that I no longer feel like a woman alone in a man's field.

This book is about the fly fishing that makes up my world. It doesn't cover all that is available, but it's a big chunk of it. My joy is primarily found in surface fishing with floating lines. Floating lines keep the fishing in the category of fun. It is not fun to dredge the bottom of a river with a fast-sinking fly line. Under circumstances that demand fishing on or near the bottom, with the possible exception of nymphing in shallow streams for trout, I'd rather use a spinning or bait-casting outfit.

Recently, artist Phyllis Sheffield, a friend who shares my love of dancing but who fishes only casually, listened patiently while I bubbled on about a recent fishing trip. "Joanie," she asked, "don't you *ever* get tired of fishing?" "No," I replied, "because it is always renewing!"

Sure, I can have enough of fishing on a tough day or in circumstances that are particularly uncomfortable, but I will never tire of what fishing gives me. It puts me in touch with another of nature's species, in beautiful surroundings that are as old as time. That is where I want to be; that is how I am renewed!

1

The Difference

From the very beginning angling has been a man's sport, but in the fifteenth century Dame Juliana Berners (whose wise counsel will be found throughout these pages) was an angler and writer. In the intervening centuries the number of women anglers has expanded only slowly, but things are changing. Twentieth-century women are finding themselves attracted to the sport for the very same reasons that it draws men. It not only offers relaxation but also the stimulation of challenge, both mental and physical, in the outdoors. Of all of the angling methods available, by which method do these newcomers to the sport choose to fish? By the method most suited to women: with a fly rod and artificial flies. Fly fishing encompasses beauty and grace to a greater degree than any other type of angling.

No other participant sport has had as much written about it as angling and the bulk of such literature is about fly fishing. Why do women need a book written especially for them? Are they lesser people who cannot understand the books written by and for men? Of course not. There are important differences, however, between male and female anglers that have not been written about.

The difference between male and female anglers is mostly physical, but there's a mental element involved too. The character of men has traditionally been more aggressive, more "predatory." I use this word as it relates to the natural world of predators and prey. Predators must outwit their prey in order to capture it because the survival of their species depends on this ability.

In sport fishing we must outwit our "prey," which are, in turn, predators too. Artificial flies are designed to appeal to that instinct within fish, and the best anglers I know are those who can most easily relate to this whole natural process. If you feel that this instinct is buried deep within you, it can be unearthed and developed and you can become a part of the natural world, as your ancestors once were. It has happened that way for me. While I may never be as good a fisherman as those whose stronger predatory instincts have given them a head start, what there is left for me in this sport is certainly all I could possibly want.

The difference between men and women that we must address is the physical one. How to measure that difference was never investigated until the armed services started to accept female recruits. In 1983 an article in *Newsweek* magazine reported that, as a result of putting male and female recruits through the same physical tests, it had been determined that women have "about" 55 percent of the strength of men, pound for pound.

Wow! If I had known that, it might have deterred me from competing with men in distance fly-casting events in which the tackle was really too heavy for me. I knew I wasn't as strong, but I could usually outcast half of my competitors. Accurate or not, 55 percent is a tough number. And there's more, from an article in *Playboy* magazine: "On the average the bodies of males are about 40 percent muscle and 15 percent fat, while the bodies of females are about 24 percent muscle and 25 percent fat. Men have wider shoulders and longer arms, they deliver oxygen to their muscles more efficiently and, pound for pound, their upper body is two to three times more powerful than a woman's." (Vol. 37 no. 4, April 1990, p. 88)

Don't let these figures discourage you. It simply means that you must use whatever strength you have as efficiently as you can, and as if that is all that is needed to enjoy the sport, because it is!

This physical difference will affect your selection of tackle. Not all tackle will be suitable for you. For instance, the rods may be too heavy and the shape and diameter of the rod grip may be too bulky. The art of casting will require more of you. The comparative limitations of your height, arm length, and strength will demand more precise movements of arm and body. Wading and playing fish will require more skill, and your gear, that which you wear and carry, must be

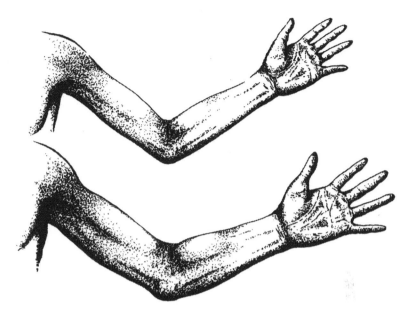

The difference in hand size and arm length between an average woman and an average man. Although physical disparities certainly exist, women can be just as successful at fly fishing.

chosen with care. Not to worry—if I can do it, you can too. This sport can be tailored to fit the individual.

Ninety percent of the women I know who love fly fishing are small, five feet five inches or less. They are, however, physically aggressive, curious about the world, and, what is most important, they are comfortable in the outdoors. They can handle heat, cold, wind, biting insects, and other discomforts without loss of dignity. When a man asks for my help in making his wife or "significant other" into a fly fisherman, I always ask, "Is she comfortable in the outdoors?" If the answer is yes, I can almost guarantee she will love this sport.

The art of fly casting always makes me think of dancing and therefore it seems more feminine than masculine. Casting has both visual beauty and a feeling of oneness in the combination of body motion, rod action, and the weight of the flexible line. Like dancing, it can make you feel beautiful, like a perfect ten on the infamous one to ten scale.

Fly fishing takes you to spectacular places and gives you a reason for being there that is far more compelling than just looking at the scenery. You become a participant rather than a spectator; the creatures of the watery world become an extension of those things you care about, almost like family and friends. It is difficult to feel lonely when you are "out fishin'."

Tying your own artificial flies broadens your participation and can add greatly to the enjoyment of the sport. The copying of standard patterns or the creation of your own designs can be both economical and satisfying. With an extensive range of natural and synthetic fly-tying materials to choose from, you are limited only by your own imagination and creativity. And there is nothing quite like the feeling that comes over you when a fish takes a fly you have tied: disbelief, then delight, and finally smug satisfaction!

There has never been a better time to be a fly fisher. There is such a wide variety of tackle and gear available that there is a good choice for everyone in any price range. The new lightweight graphite rods are a fisherwoman's delight. You'll find attractive and functional clothing, hats, and vests. Waders are weighed in ounces now instead of pounds, and neoprene waders, for cold-weather fishing, are the closest we can come to stretch pants. Sexy.

Fly fishing is a lifetime sport. You can leave it to raise children and come back to it when you once again have time to devote to it. It won't have lost any of its luster. Of course, the younger you are when you begin, the better, while your eyes are in their best condition. There is lots to see: a sipping trout, hatching insects, a fish taking your fly at a distance. Being able to tie tiny trout flies onto fine leader tippets when your eyes are getting older is not nearly so difficult if you have had practice at an earlier age.

This is also a sport that strengthens relationships. If you can fish with someone, you can probably live with them happily. Fishing is a test of your values. Most fly fishermen are thoughtful, sensitive, caring individuals. All the single ones I know, men or women, are looking for mates who will love to fish as much as they do.

Fly fishing can be a complex sport, but it needn't be. This book is meant to guide you through the forest by pointing out the trees that are most important to you, as a "fisherwoman," in finding your way. To get the most out of this sport you must be independent: capable of choosing your tackle, tying on leader tippets and flies, reading water, wading safely, and playing fish with skill. You must know how to release a fish unharmed or how to kill it swiftly so that it doesn't suffer.

Other anglers will give you some of their time, when you need help, but fishing time is precious and you shouldn't ask for more than a little. You may better understand this when time spent fly fishing becomes precious to you, too.

2

Our Heritage

In 1496 the *Treatise of Fishing with an Angle,* the first extant work ever printed in English on the subject of sport fishing, was published. Its authorship has been attributed to a woman, Dame Juliana Berners. She did exist as a writer or compiler and her name is firmly attached to the first hunting treatise printed in English (first *Book of St. Albans,* 1486). When the hunting treatise was printed a second time (second *Book of St. Albans,* 1496), the fishing treatise was included.

John McDonald, whose *Origins of Angling* (Doubleday, 1963) is the best historical reference to date, writes that the fishing treatise is "strictly speaking, anonymous" and of Dame Juliana:

"She was, as the legend goes, noble in birth and spirit, sociable, solitary, dashing, beautiful, learned, and intellectual. In some accounts she fled to field sports to avoid love; in another she might have retired to a convent 'from disappointment.' . . . The seeming conflict between nun and sportswoman together with the scarcity of evidence for assertions made about her, have been the cause of spirited argument among generations of antiquaries."

McDonald goes on to say that it is the anglers who have adopted her as the author and that she is still the only candidate.

I have included a copy of her treatise in the appendix and extracts from it appear throughout the book. I think you will find, as I have, that because of the turn of phrase it is easy to believe that it was written by a woman. Remember that, in those days, the word "man" meant everyone. What man, though, would suggest, for instance, that to take care of hornets, bumblebees, and wasps for bait, one should bake them in bread? She also suggests feeding maggots with mutton fat and with a cake made of flour and honey and to keep them in a *"bag of blanket, kept hot under your gown or other warm thing."* No man would say this, would he?

Join me in believing, and let Dame Juliana's spirit be with you always, with thoughts like these:

> *Solomon in his Proverbs says that a good spirit makes a flowering age, that is, a fair age and a long one. And since it is so, I ask this question, "What are the means and the causes that lead a man into a merry spirit?" Truly, in my best judgment, it seems that they are good sports and honest games in which a man takes pleasure without any repentance afterward. Thence it follows that good recreations and honorable pastimes are the cause of a man's fair old age and long life.*

To Juliana the best of all recreations is angling, *"a merry occupation, without care, anxiety or trouble, which may rejoice his heart and in which his spirits may have a merry delight."* In fishing

> *the angler can have no cold nor discomfort nor anger, unless he be the cause himself. For he can lose at the most only a line or a hook, of which he can have a plentiful supply of his own making . . . So then his loss is not grievous, and other griefs he cannot have, except that some fish may break away after he has been caught on the hook, or else that he may catch nothing. These are not grievous, for if the angler fails with one, he may not fail with another, if he does as this treatise teaches—unless there are no fish in the water. And yet, at the very least, he has his wholesome and merry walk at his ease, and a sweet breath of the sweet smell of the meadow flowers, that makes him hungry. He hears the*

melodious harmony of birds. He sees the young swans, herons, ducks, coots, and many other birds with their broods . . . And if the angler catches fish, surely then there is no man merrier than he is in his spirit.

How very well this is said, and I agree with her that it is more the fishing than the catching at which we anglers spend our time and by which we are renewed, but it is the catching that makes our spirits really soar.

On this side of the Atlantic things were, obviously, quite undeveloped in the fifteenth century. It isn't until the nineteenth century that we next see a woman's name and it is on an extraordinary subject: entomology. Sara Jane McBride learned fly fishing and fly tying from her father, professional tyer John McBride of Monroe County, New York. After studying the year-round insect cycle of shallow, food-rich Spring Creek, near Caledonia, Sara wrote the first published American papers of any consequence on the subject of aquatic insects from an angler's perspective. The articles appeared in *Forest and Stream* in 1876 and *Rod and Gun* in 1877. The fly-fishing fraternity, as a whole, didn't have a clue about insect life and most fly patterns were what we now call "attractors." Sara's flies, which won her a bronze medal at the Centennial Exposition in 1876, were imitations of naturals. She also observed the importance of water temperature and the effects that even a degree or two of change could have on pupae and larvae in the bed of Spring Creek. She was way ahead of her time.

Cornelia "Fly Rod" Crosby is the firecracker of our ancestors. She gave us a real boost. Born in 1854 in Phillips, Maine, she grew up with a rod and gun in her hands and was issued Maine Guide License #1. She did what has been extremely difficult for man or woman to do: She made her living by fishing and writing about it in her column "Fly Rod's Notebook" in the nationally distributed publication *The Maine Woods*. As a representative of the Maine Central Railroad she evaluated lodges and hotels, covering what was new and who caught the biggest fish where, and her appearances at sportsmen's shows in New York and Boston drew record crowds. She was acknowledged to be the most famous fly fisherwoman in the world. And this was in the 1890s!

Fly tying is the area of our sport in which women have been most involved and influential. The standardization of fly patterns came about mainly through the efforts of fly tyer Mary Orvis Marbury, the daughter of Charles F. Orvis, founder of the famous Vermont tackle company. Houghton Mifflin Company published Ms. Marbury's book, *Favorite Flies and Their Histories*, in 1892. It was a compilation of information contributed by Orvis's customers and, with twenty-two color plates of 290 patterns, was the most lavish and beautiful angling book of its time. Mary's execution of this project has given her a place in fly-fishing history as an angling author.

Carrie Frost of Stevens Point, Wisconsin, started commercial fly tying in 1890 by hiring a few girls to work under her direction. Stevens Point became the fly-tying capital of the world and, in the mid-1940s, women working in factories were turning out ten million flies each year.

Many women who tie flies commercially have no interest in fishing, but one who did was a milliner in the Rangeley Lakes region of Maine. In 1924, Carrie Stevens changed the way streamers were to be tied after she caught a 6-pound 13-ounce brook trout in the Upper Dam pool on one of her "homemade" flies. Her fish took second place in that year's *Field & Stream* fishing contest and captured the attention of the eastern trout-fishing world. The look of streamers changed from high wings on short-shank hooks to long wings, parallel to the shank, on a long-shank hook. Carrie's original smelt imitation developed into the forever popular Gray Ghost streamer.

Elizabeth Greig was another tyer who loved fly fishing. Born in Scotland, she served four years of apprenticeship as a fly dresser before coming to the United States in 1930. Greig tied for Jim Deren's Angler's Roost in New York City and her claim to fame was that her flies (and they were top of the line) were tied in her fingers, without a vise.

Helen Shaw Kessler's professional tying career began in Wisconsin but continues today in East Chatham, New York. Helen is also an exceptional teacher of the art, as shown in her books *Fly Tying: Materials, Tools, Technique* and *Flies for Fish and Fishermen*.

In the early 1900s, Ferdon's River View Inn, on the Beaverkill in Roscoe, New York, was a home away from home for fly fishermen, as well as the birthplace of the owner's granddaughter, Winnie Ferdon Dette. Constantly in the company of fishermen as she was growing up, Winnie had only a casual interest in fishing itself until she started to date Walter Dette. The two, along with Walt's friend Harry Darbee, became a fishing threesome, then, as a team, turned to fly tying in 1927, using the hotel as the outlet for their first commercial sales.

Walt and Winnie married in 1928, and the business grew to the point where, in 1934, a local girl named Elsie Bivins was hired to sort hackles and other materials. Harry taught Elsie to become a "professional tyer of high quality flies" and, soon after, they were married.

The group split and the Dettes and Darbees, separately, became the main practitioners of the Catskill style of fly tying.

In addition to running a thriving business, the Darbees made a name for themselves in the 1960s by fighting conservation battles, from dams and highways to aerial spraying. The Dettes worked at other jobs in order to educate their two children but today, sixty-odd years from the time they began, they are still tying flies in their Cottage Street home in Roscoe, having been joined in 1954 by their daughter Mary Clark. The flies of all three are exactly alike and the flies are simply "Dette flies." The mother-to-daughter tradition has only a slight chance of being carried on by Mary's daughter Linda, but it would certainly be nice for the Catskill school of fly tying to have a bloodline continuity.

In the five hundred years since Dame Juliana's time, the women who have gained notoriety in this field can be counted on two hands: McBride, Crosby, Marbury, Frost, Stevens, Greig, Darbee, Shaw, and Dette. The good news is that we can be proud of every one of them. We are not starting from scratch; we have a heritage!

3

The Clubs and Organizations

Clubs and organizations can play an important part in the life of an angler. "Private-water" clubs offer a limited membership of compatible anglers and well-stocked fishing waters. Their general purpose is relaxation and fun. Open-membership organizations, on the other hand, offer education in the form of clinics, a chance to make friends with other fishermen, and the opportunity to be involved in preserving and protecting the sport through conservation projects. Many anglers are members of both types of associations.

In the Northeast, the private-water clubs started forming in the mid-1800s. No ladies, please, was the general order of the day with a few exceptions. The Southside Sportsman's Club, established in 1866 on the Connetquot River on Long Island, allowed ladies to stay in two annex buildings but did not permit them in the clubhouse itself. Believe it or not, the Beaverkill Trout Club in the Catskills still feels that way, allowing ladies to enter only one of the two buildings. The fishing wife of a male member may fish, but I know of another Catskill club that turned down a friend for membership for the very reason that his wife fished. *That* was seen as potential trouble! There are, however, a couple of Catskill clubs that do take women as members.

In 1897, Pennsylvania's Blooming Grove Club was more enlightened and welcomed lady anglers. "The presence of women, no matter where, is elevating," read one of their brochures. "It retards nothing in the conduct of all self-respecting men."

The year 1932 saw the establishment of the Woman Flyfisher's Club. It was started by Julia Fairchild, wife of the then president of the all-male New York Angler's Club. The Angler's Club is not limited to fly fishing but this new club was. The stated goal was "to cultivate, further, and practice the art of scientific angling; to acquire by lease, purchase, or otherwise, a clubhouse with grounds and water thereon, as a resort for fishing and shooting; to encourage contests of skill in fly casting; to encourage in all ways the protection and propagation of fish and game."

Julia, who in the later years of her long life (she lived beyond the age of ninety-five) came to be called Dame Juliana by her clubmates, was joined by many other extraordinary women. There were thirty-three of them that first year. Among them were Mabel Ingalls and Jane Smith, and all three women brought their own strong sense of conservation to the group. The club has been effective in bringing issues to public attention and in getting politicians to pay attention to conservation concerns. Over the years the Woman Flyfishers did get a clubhouse on a Catskill stream, thereby becoming a private-water club.

The first woman's fishing "organization" is the International Women's Fishing Association (IWFA), with headquarters in Palm Beach, Florida. It allows any and all kinds of fishing within its rules. It was chartered in 1955 by Denny Crowninshield, Kay Rybovitch, Ginny Sherwood, and Jackie Gerli. Its goals were "to go fishing" and to be shown the same consideration in competition that was reserved for men. The group is not politically active but the membership is kept apprised of conservation issues. Additionally, the IWFA has set up a scholarship in the field of marine education.

Big-game fishing is the major interest of IWFA's membership, but its activities also include other game fish such as trout, salmon, bass, and bonefish. There is a fly-fishing division in the monthly and yearly competitions for released and weighed fish. IWFA has been good for women who want to prove their capabilities through competition.

The Golden West Women Fly Fishers was born in the 1980s, having been conceived by Fanny Krieger and Susan Williams of San Francisco. The group consists mostly of working women who love to fish and also like to share the experience with other women. They have *fun*! Monthly meetings offer guest-speaker programs, along with wine and goodies (for a small fee). There are also several outings and clinics each year. All is chronicled in a monthly newsletter. The cause of conservation seems to hit a responsive chord in women, and this group, too, publicizes and helps solve problems, sometimes holding fund-raising events for fishing-related causes.

I am a member of Golden West and thoroughly enjoy the air of camaraderie and conviviality so apparent when I am able to visit. I've always been a bit envious of the members of male clubs and here's the answer. We need a group in the East as soon as we can think of a better name than Acid Rain East Fly Fishers, although many dedicated women here already belong to the Theodore Gordon Flyfishers. TGF is known as perhaps the most potent conservation club in the country. Along with an Arts of Angling series each winter, there's a luncheon gathering every Tuesday, often including a fly-fishing travel program, at a university club in New York City.

Clubs like those above and chapters of national organizations, such as Trout Unlimited (TU) and the Federation of Fly Fishers (FFF), can do two important things for you. First, they put you in touch with others who love to fish and from whom you can learn. Second, they give you a vehicle through which you can give something back to the sport, whether it is by donation, physical work to improve a stream, or letters to your political representatives. Giving back to a sport you love, especially one that depends on a clean environment, not only makes you feel good but is thought of by many anglers as a responsibility.

It's not a new idea. In the fifteenth century, our role model, Dame Juliana, wrote:

> *Also, you must not be too greedy in catching your said game, as in taking too much at one time . . . That could easily be the occasion of destroying your own sport and other men's also. When you have a sufficient mess, you should covet no more at that time. Also you should busy yourself to nourish the game in everything that you can, and to destroy all such things as are devourers of it.*

Amen.

4

The Tools: Fly-fishing Tackle

If you want to be crafty in angling, you must first learn to make your tackle . . . You must cut, between Michaelmas and Candlemas [September 29 to February 2], a fair staff . . . of hazel, willow, or aspen; and soak it in a hot oven, and set it straight. Then let it cool and dry for a month. . . . bind it to a bench . . . take a plumber's wire . . . heat the sharp end in a charcoal fire . . . and burn the staff through with it . . . Then let it lie still and cool for two days. Untie it then and let it dry in a house-roof . . . [And for the tip] take a fair rod of green hazel and soak it even and straight, and let it dry with the staff.

Before the first fiberglass rods were manufactured in 1947, and with the exception of a few ungainly models made of steel, all fly-fishing rods were handmade of wood. "Lovingly crafted" is the way I prefer to think of it. Bill Taylor, my distance-casting mentor, made his own rods in a room behind his "sundries" shop, and they were his life's passion. I remember waiting for him to create my distance rod. It took months. Choosing the cane, planing, baking, resting, fitting ferrules, winding on the guides with silk thread and, finally, finishing with several coats of fine varnish was a labor of love. It still is.

Because we have other options, not too many of us will consider making a rod from scratch, but most rod companies offer blanks to be wrapped and finished at home. Anglers willing to put in the time can save money or personalize a rod in the color and pattern of the wrappings, and in choosing the reel seat.

In both ready-made rods or blanks, today's state-of-the-art material is third-generation graphite (carbon fibers), but good fly rods are available in the earlier graphites and in glass and bamboo. The factors involved in choosing a rod are these: first, the species of fish to be caught and then, within that category and your price range, the line weight, rod weight, action and length, and configuration of the rod grip.

In terms of cost, glass is the least expensive, and graphites, which are combinations of glass and graphite, are next. The higher the ratio of graphite to glass, the more expensive the rod. Bamboo rods by the top craftsmen are the most costly. Some bamboo rods are so expensive they are bought as investments and never used for fishing.

Your most important determination will be the rod weight. Graphite is the lightest to handle a given line weight; bamboo and glass are very similar to each other. Third-generation graphite benefits all anglers but is particularly exciting for women. Lighter than other graphites, the rods also have exceptional quickness, sending the fly line to its target with almost no undulation or wavering, as has been so common in the past. I'm really high on these new graphites and in love with particular models, because they make casting more pleasurable. Each cast is more likely to be perfect with less effort. You'll find them under various designations, according to the manufacturer: Graphite III, IM7, IMX, HLS, and so on. They are also available in four-piece travel models.

Rods suitable for various species range in length from 6 to 10 feet and in weight from less than two ounces, for trout, to five or six ounces for tarpon or billfish. Each rod is designed to cast a specific line weight, which is designated by a number between 1 and 12.

The first thirty feet of the fly line is weighed in grains and designated accordingly. A #6 line, for instance, weighs between 152 and 168 grains; a #10 is between 270 and 290 grains. The line-weight number a rod is designed to cast can be found imprinted on the butt section, above the grip. Fly fishermen speak of rods by that line-weight number: a 6-weight rod, a 10-weight rod, and so on.

Choose your tackle, for a particular species, based on the range of fly sizes to be used and the general conditions under which you must cast them. Are the flies light or heavy? Is there constant wind to contend with? Will you fish on large streams or small ones? Will you be wading or fishing from a boat? Answers to these questions will give you a starting point from which you'll work backward, choosing the line weight first and then a rod to match it.

Line Weight

The following range of line weights for various species includes the lightest and heaviest weights commonly used by anglers of both sexes. The weight and/or air resistance of the flies, the distance they must be cast, and the factor of wind that may be encountered is the basis for the table. Be aware that the weight of the rod will increase as the line weight increases. It is a good idea to start at the light end of the range in all types of fishing with the exception of trout.

Line Weights for Fish Species	
Trout	#1 to #8
Bass	#7 to #10
Atlantic salmon	#6 to #10
Bonefish/Permit	#6 to #9
Tarpon	#9 to #12
Billfish	#9 to #12
Saltwater school fish	#8 to #10

There are eight line weights suitable for trout fishing. I consider #6 to be the all-purpose line weight. It will be suitable under most conditions, except in heavy winds, even with weighted flies. Small flies are accommodated by tapering the leader to a very fine tippet, which is the last piece of monofilament before the fly. There is enough weight in a #6 line to give beginners a feeling of the subtle weight of the fly line on the cast, something extremely difficult to sense with the #1, #2, and #3 weights. A rod that will cast a 6-weight line can weigh three ounces or less, which is the weight limit I suggest for trout.

I realize that some women have very little hand strength and that even a 6-weight rod is too much rod. Then start with a #5, or even a #4. The #4 and #5 handicap you slightly in wind or with weighted flies, but if it is all you can handle, start there. Don't use any lighter weights until you have fishing experience and know exactly why you want one of them.

The line table shows species other than trout and, wherever it is appropriate, my fishing is done with the same #6 rod. With it I use either a standard weight-forward #6 line or a triangle taper #6/7 line. The need for heavier lines and rods is determined by the weight or bulkiness of the flies and the wind. Bass bugs, for example, are bulky and air resistant so they require a fairly heavy line to push them through the air. Tarpon are enormous fish and can weigh up to 200 pounds. A heavier rod and line are needed to cast the heavier flies and a rod with some stiffness in the butt section helps when you're fighting such a large fish. The rod must also accommodate the large reel required to hold 250 yards of backing line in addition to the fly line.

Atlantic salmon, bonefish, and permit can all be taken on #6 outfits. If the wind blows, though, you have to be a better caster to keep up with the conditions than if you were relying on brute strength with the heavier outfits. As you develop the hand and fore-arm strength to cast the #6 outfit, you can begin to work with heavier tackle for the few times you might need it. I travel with a 6-weight outfit for these species but back myself up with a #8/9 for heavier flies and tough wind conditions. This rod weighs 3½ ounces in the new graphite. For tarpon fishing I use a 10-weight rod weighing 4⅜ ounces (in older graphite) but use it with a #11 line. There is no way I will ever be able to master a 12-weight rod, unless one of the new graphites can do it for me.

The bottom line here is that you can cast a heavy outfit for short periods of time, such as when tarpon fishing, because you cast only when you have spotted fish, which may be moving with the tide. On the other hand, in stream fishing, such as for trout or salmon, the fish remain in their lies and you are fishing all of the likely water, making hundreds of casts in a day. The tackle you choose must do its job well and be light enough to let you maintain peak performance without tiring.

Line Design

The next decision, after choosing the weight of your fly line, is that of choosing the design of the line. Standard fly lines are at least ninety feet long. The effective weight, for casting them, is spread throughout the length on some designs and concentrated in the front thirty to forty feet in others. On the line design chart you'll find a measurement guide to the length of the various sections that may be tapered or remain level, and may be thick (for more weight) or thin (for less weight). Learn the vocabulary: point, front taper, belly, back taper, and shooting or running line. The word "head" is commonly used on weight-forward-type lines to denote the entire weighted section (front taper, belly, and back taper).

Note: Line manufacturers now and then change the configuration of their designs. Use the dimensions shown on the chart only as a guide.

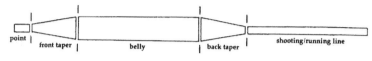

Parts of a Fly Line

Level

This design has no taper. It is better for trolling than for casting, although it could be used for bass fishing or any other fishing in which heavy leaders and flies are used and there is no need for delicate presentations. The potential for the technique of shooting line is limited with level lines.

Double Taper

Tapered at both ends so that it can be reversed when one end wears

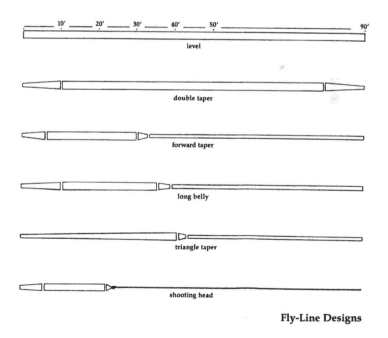

Fly-Line Designs

out, this line with its eight to ten feet of front taper will help to present your flies delicately. This design is the traditional trout-fishing line. Its only limitation is that, because of the seventy-foot belly portion (where the diameter remains constant), its long cast potential is not as easily reached as with a weight-forward line.

Weight Forward
On this design, the front taper is six to eight feet long, followed by the belly section of twenty-two to twenty-four feet for a total of thirty feet of weight. The remaining sixty feet is running/shooting line. Once the thirty-foot "head" is out of the rod tip, the lighter shooting line behind it becomes a string tail on a thirty-foot "rock" and gives full long-cast potential. This line can be used for trout fishing. Variations on this taper are made for specific species such as bass, bonefish, tarpon, or just "salt water."

Long-belly Weight Forward
A combination of the double taper and the forward taper, this line incorporates the best characteristics of each. It includes the long front taper and some of the longer belly of the double taper, but is in the weight-forward configuration, which includes running line for long-cast capabilities.

Triangle Taper
This consists of one continuous taper for the length of the weighted section, which varies from twenty-seven to forty feet long before tapering to the shooting line. (Heavier sizes have shorter weighted sections to balance heavier flies.) There is no belly. The name comes from the elongated triangle shape of the weighted section when drawn on paper. It is based on the original English fly-line design, when fly lines were braided of horsehairs and tapered continuously. An excellent line for roll casting, it has a delicate front taper in the sizes suitable for trout fishing. The triangle taper's shooting capabilities are like other weight-forward tapers except that the shooting line is smaller in diameter for less air resistance.

Shooting Head
A twenty- to thirty-foot head, or weighted section, which the angler then attaches to monofilament shooting line, is suitable for fishing under conditions where maximum distance is necessary. It requires dexterity to hold this shooting line in loops, not only with your line hand but perhaps between your teeth also, or you can buy a waist-slung canvas basket made expressly for holding the monofilament.

This design is used for trout, salmon, or steelhead on big rivers where eighty- to one hundred-foot casts are the norm.

Fly-line Color

> *After you have made your rod, you must learn to color your lines of hair in this manner. First you must take, from the tail of a white horse, the longest and best hair that you can find, and the rounder it is, the better it is. Divide it into six bunches, and you must color every part by itself in a different color, such as yellow, green, brown, tawny, russet and dusky colors. . . . To make your hair yellow . . . take a half-gallon of small ale, and crush three handfuls of walnut leaves . . . put in your hair till it is as deep a yellow as you want to have it.*
>
> *When your hair is thus colored, you must know for which waters and for which seasons they will serve. The green color in all clear water from April till September. The yellow color in every clear water from September till November, for it is like the weeds and other kinds of grass which grow in the waters and rivers . . . The russet color serves for all the winter until the end of April, as well in rivers as in pools and lakes. [Use] brown . . . [in] water that is black, sluggish . . . tawny color for those waters that are heathy or marshy.*

Juliana Berners tied her fly directly to the fly line so its color was extremely important. Now anglers use tapered monofilament leaders, which are an invisible extension of the fly line, on which they tie their fly. Color is immaterial because a good fisherman never lets the fish see the line. However, the visibility of white lines, or other bright colors, provides a reference as to accuracy of the cast and the fly's location in poor light conditions.

Rod Action

The word "action" describes how the rod bends and how quickly it straightens after the cast. If a rod wiggles or vibrates for one or two seconds after the cast has been made, it means that much of the force you put into the rod was dissipated on its transfer to the line and was wasted. A rod that is "fast," or "quick," and that bends progressively, starting with a relatively stiff butt section and gradually becoming

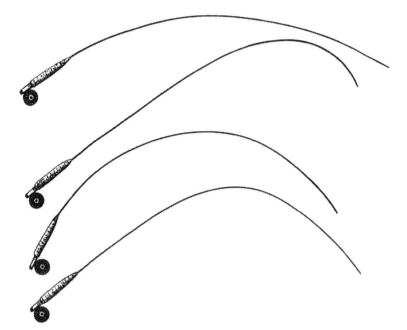

Rod actions, top to bottom: progressive, tip, too soft, and hinging.

more bendable, is the kind most experienced anglers like to work with. This action doesn't waste the caster's energy as it is transferred to the fly line but, instead, adds to it.

A softer progressive action, one in which the rod's bend can be felt all the way down to the grip and which does not "dampen" quickly, is sometimes more effective for beginners than are faster actions. The slower action also contributes to softer presentations, which are desirable when fishing very small flies on long leaders to wary trout. Whatever your preference though, two rod actions to avoid are those combining very stiff butt sections with very limber tip sections, which give a feeling of "hinging," and "parabolic" actions that combine a soft butt, stiff middle section, and a soft tip. Rods of this latter action can magnify the least little error in your casting to make you doubly unhappy with the results.

"Well," you ask, "how am I ever going to find my way through the maze of rods available?" Very simply. After choosing the line-weight category, look at the rods in your price range that will match that weight. The next step is to cast several rods before making your decision. Once you have tried two rods of different actions you will be able to discriminate between them, liking one better than the other. The rod action that is best for you, of all those you try, will effect your casting immediately—it will improve it to give you results you were not sure you could expect. You'll know which one to choose so trust yourself!

Rod Length

A misconception that works against women in fly fishing is that short people should use short fly rods. It's really just the opposite. What the rod lacks in length the caster has to make up for with longer strokes. Stroke length is limited by arm length. Short people have short arms. Logic class—the shorter you are, the more a longer rod will do for you.

For all fishing other than trout fishing, 9-foot-long rods are the standard length. For trout, because of the various widths of the rivers and streams, experienced anglers can choose from the full range of rod lengths, from 6 to 10 feet long. Nevertheless, unless most of your fishing will be done on very small streams where a shorter rod will be no handicap, begin with a rod that is in the 8- to 9-foot class, taking into consideration your arm length and the overall weight of the rod.

Short rods require more of the caster, even if you are tall. Because the line is always traveling at a fairly low level and gravity is waiting in the wings to pull it down to the water, greater line speed has to be generated. So short rods are a challenge, but think about them for sometime in the future, when you have learned to cast well. They can be pure pleasure. I learned to use a 6-foot rod during the fiberglass era. An 8½- or 9-foot rod weighed 3½ to 4 ounces and any fishing trip longer than a day became an endurance test. My hand would hurt, and I still wear the scars of calluses at the base of my fingers. The 6-foot rods of glass or bamboo weighed less than 2 ounces but cast 6- or 7-weight lines and changed agony to pleasure on long fishing days.

Rod Grips

The diameter and shape of the rod's cork grip is another factor that can make the difference between pleasure and pain. This is the rule: The grip must be compatible with the size and shape of your hand. During the casting stroke you hold the grip firmly as you accelerate the rod to a sudden stop. To stop it, you squeeze/clutch it by suddenly contracting your hand and arm muscles. Then you relax and start the process in the other direction. Your hand is working constantly, so if the diameter of the grip is too large, or swells in the wrong place, you'll suffer for it. When you are choosing your fly rod, check the different shapes of grips available; if you cannot get what you want, sandpaper may solve the problem. Cork can be sanded away to give you a more comfortable fit.

I believe that one of the reasons women have been "turned off" by fly fishing in the past is that they have depended on men to choose their tackle. As a consequence, their rods have been too heavy and sometimes unwieldy. This can result in real physical discomforts like skin burns on the heel of the hand and a sore thumb, as well as a general feeling of helplessness in trying to control the rod.

Countless couples have come to me for casting instruction with the woman using the heavier of their two outfits. He bought a new rod for its "great action" and perhaps its lightness, but because the old one didn't tire him in any way and was as comfortable as an old shoe (he learned with it) he thinks he's doing her a favor by giving something of himself, something he was happy with, to help her get started. He doesn't realize the importance of weight because he has nearly twice her strength to begin with and has gained additional hand strength by doing the many manual chores that have traditionally been in men's domain.

Because our traditional manual chores, like wringing clothes, squeezing oranges, and holding brushes to scrub floors, have been lightened by electrical appliances, women don't develop much hand strength unless they do it in sport. So don't feel bad and don't be surprised if his feelings are hurt when, upon reading on his gift trout rod that it weighs 3½ ounces, you tell him you need something lighter.

Rod companies sometimes offer models that have been "designed for women." Remember that they have usually been designed for women by men. Don't buy them blindly. Check out their weight, the rod grip, and the action. Do this even when you are told that a woman designed them. Do this even if Joan Wulff designed them.

No one else can or should choose a rod for you.

Reels

I choose fly reels that are light and durable, in the smallest size that will hold the fly line and the amount of backing I will need. (Backing is braided Dacron line that goes on the reel under your fly line and comes into use when a fish runs farther than the ninety feet of your fly line's length.) I don't use a drag, which is an adjustable mechanical brake on the reel spool, so there's no need to pay for that machining or to carry the extra weight a drag adds. The reel must have a "click," however, so that it doesn't overrun when a hooked fish surges or runs the line off the spool at great speed.

Choose your reel with the weight factor in mind. On each cast you make you start the whole outfit from a dead stop and accelerate it to another dead stop. The heavier the reel, the more energy you must use and the more hand strength you must have.

Fly reels have traditionally been wound with the right hand by right-handed anglers. I have my reels converted for left-hand winding so that I may use the rod more capably when playing large or difficult fish. My right arm has more strength, it is cued to my dominant eye, and it will respond more quickly when reflex action is called for. My left hand learned to go around in a circle, guided by the reeling mechanism, in two short fishing sessions. It is primarily a mental adjustment. You might consider this and have your reel converted at the time of purchase.

Leaders

With How Many Hairs You Must Angle For Each Fish

For the minnow, with a line of one hair. For the growing roach, the bleak, the gudgeon, and the ruff, with a line of two hairs. For the dace and the great roach, with a line of three hairs. For the perch, the flounder, and small bream, with four hairs. For the chevin-chub, the bream, the tench, and the eel, with six hairs. For the trout, grayling, barbel, and the great chevin, with nine hairs. . . . For the salmon, with fifteen hairs.

The strength of Dame Juliana's fly line has been transposed, over time, to the strength and/or diameter of our leaders. The monofilament leader is the invisible and weightless continuation of the fly line. It must taper from roughly two-thirds of the diameter of the line's tip end to whatever diameter is suitable for the size of the fly being used. Its strength (measured in pound-test) must be relative to the weight of the fish you expect to encounter. Anglers refer to the "strength" of the whole outfit by the strength of the weakest section of leader, that which is next to the fly.

The flies used for salmon, steelhead, bass, and saltwater species are all fairly large, so the leaders needed to cast them are only six to nine feet long. For these fish they are usually referred to in pound-test designations such as 6-pound test, 8-pound test, and so on. Trout leaders are different. They are referred to by the diameter of the thin-

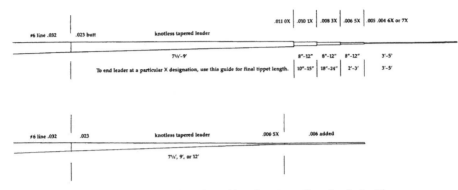

Tapered trout leaders. Top: combination of knotless taper (base leader) with
custom tapering of front end. Bottom: knotless taper to desired X designation plus
additional tippet.

nest section of leader (the part next to the fly), for example, 3X, 5X,
and so on.

When fishing for trout with streamers, wet flies, or weighted
nymphs, the leader can be relatively short because the fly, cast quartering downstream, comes to the fish ahead of the leader. When fly
fishing upstream with dry flies or weightless nymphs, however, you
need careful leader construction: length, gentle tapering, and invisi-
bility become extremely important.

Diameters above .011 (eleven thousandths of an inch) are designated just that way: .023, .021, .017, and so on. From .011 downward,
though, an X-system is introduced: .011 becomes 0X, .010 is 1X, .009 is
2X, and so on, down to the smallest, 8X, or .003. The X number and
the actual diameter add up to 11.

Although you can construct your own leaders from sections of
monofilament of different diameters, I suggest that you buy knotless
tapers and add to them. My base leader is a knotless taper that ends in
0X or 1X. Then, from the spools of 1X, 3X, 5X, and 6X or 7X tippet
material I carry in my vest, I taper and build the rest of the leader to
conform to the size of my fly and the way I want to present it.

The smallest diameter, that of the tippet section next to the fly, can
be determined by this general guide: Divide the hook size by four to
get the X designation. If your fly is tied on a #12 hook, taper the leader
down to 3X tippet. A #20 will need a 5X, or .006, diameter. The leader
must taper gradually. You can't tie 5X to 0X and expect it to cast well
because it will hinge and collapse on itself. Taper it with 8- to 12-inch-

long pieces of tippet. Drop down in diameter .002, or two X-designations, at a time until you reach the final tippet section next to the fly.

Make that final piece of tippet longer. As you go down in strength, go up in length. A characteristic of monofilament is that it stretches. With a short leader tippet of fine diameter, the shock of a trout's jumps and surges is much more likely to use up that stretch and break it than it might with a longer one. The additional stretch acts as a cushion for these shocks. Also, longer tippets will help present tiny flies more naturally. As a guide, with a 5X tippet, use two to three feet, and with a 6 or 7X tippet, three to five. If it doesn't straighten, it will be a better presentation.

You also have the option of buying a ready-made leader tapered to whatever X designation you want next to the fly. But if, for example, you buy a nine-foot leader tapered to 5X, modify it by adding more 5X to be sure the tippet length is adequate.

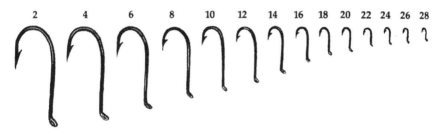

Life-size hook chart

Leaders

Size	Tip Diameter	Tip Test
7X	.004	2 lbs.
6X	.005	3 lbs.
5X	.006	4 lbs.
4X	.007	5 lbs.
3X	.008	6 lbs.
2X	.009	7 lbs.
1X	.010	9 lbs.
0X	.011	10 lbs.

Knots

Knots are relatively easy for women to learn because of our innate and inherited ability to be good with our hands. Like all other skills, however, getting them into the memory bank permanently requires practice. When you first learn a knot, keep some monofilament near the television or some other "sitting" spot and practice when your hands are otherwise idle. If you have difficulty tying them because of the small diameters, start with rope or large-diameter monofilament and then work down to the finer sizes.

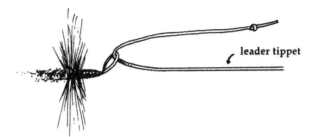

Clinch Knot. Thread leader through the hook eye and make an overhand knot at the end.

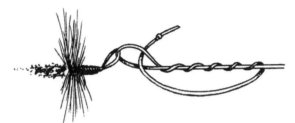

Make five turns with the end around the leader. Bring the overhand knot through loop at eye.

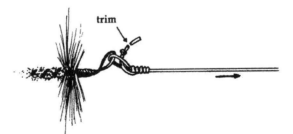

Hold the knot against the hook eye. Pull the leader stem away from the fly and wraps will jam against the hook eye. Trim the end carefully—not so close as to lose the overhand knot.

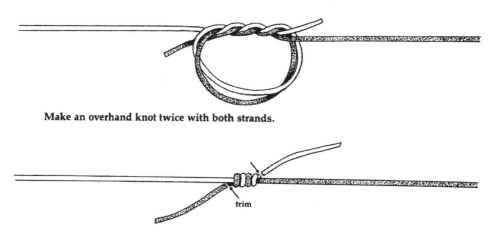

Surgeon's Knot. Overlap the two strands of leader to be tied.

Make an overhand knot twice with both strands.

trim

Hold both strands on both sides, slowly pull the knot tight, and trim the ends.

There are many books written and illustrated on the subject of knots but you may find them easier to learn from a friendly fisherman. Here are three knots you'll need in order to set up your tackle— the first is used to tie on a fly, the second to tie pieces of leader tippet together, and the third to attach your leader to the fly line.

Clinch Knot

The overhand knot in the end of the leader ensures that the clinch will not slip out. It is both safer and easier than the Improved Clinch Knot most anglers use.

Surgeon's Knot

This is not as symmetrically beautiful as the Barrel or Blood Knot but is simpler. It may also be a few percentage points weaker. Learn the Blood Knot eventually. I use this one with fine diameters after I've missed the Blood Knot three times.

Jam Knot

This is in place of the more complicated (but smoother and more durable) Needle Knot, which attaches the leader to the end of the fly line. There must be a loop in the end of the leader for this one.

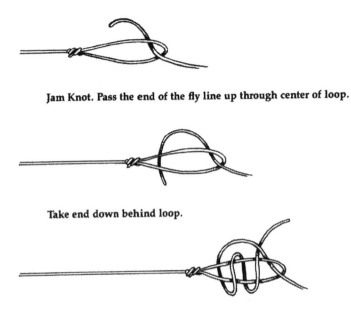

Jam Knot. Pass the end of the fly line up through center of loop.

Take end down behind loop.

Wrap end twice around loop only.

Hold end of fly line and slowly draw knot tight. Trim.

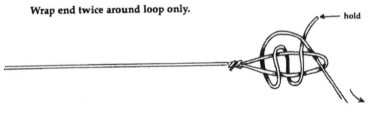

5

To Cast a Fly

If you like dancing, in any of its forms, and then you learn to fly cast, you may notice similarities between the two. Both include graceful body movement. Parts of the body sometimes move independently within movement of the whole. Both can be done in time with music. There are changes in tempo, beauty of form, and lots of feeling.

Feeling—that's the bottom line. That's why fly casting is so right for women. You dance from your toes to your fingertips and, although you are standing in one spot, you fly cast from your toes to your fingertips. But there is more to it than just your body, and that is the addition of the fly rod's action. The movement of your body and arm brings the rod to life to interact with the fly line. Fly casting is a flow of energy that moves from your hand to the rod and from the rod to the line in a fleeting instant of intense feeling. The energy then takes its final form in the gracefully unrolling fly-line loop, your visual reward for having done it well.

In all other sports the moment of impact separates you from the very thing you are projecting in beautiful flight (baseball is a good example of this). The execution of a perfect cast, however, can be seen

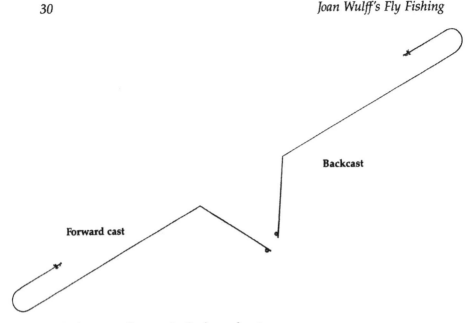

The backcast unrolls opposite the forward cast.

and felt from its inception until the fly touches down on the water.

It takes a while to reach this rewarding stage of fly casting, just as it does in dancing. You first learn the "steps," and then you practice until one move flows smoothly into the next. I often combine fly casting and dancing with Fly-O, a 3-foot-long indoor practice rod (which uses gift-wrap yarn for fly line) and some of my favorite music. I free-form dance while casting, or just keeping the yarn in motion, in time with the music.

Fly casting is different from all other sports in that each cast requires not just one, but *two strokes*: a backcast and a forward cast. In all other sports you set up slowly on the backswing and then hit or throw something forward. Baseball, tennis, and golf are good examples of one-stroke sports. Fly casting's two strokes require that the same speed and force be used on the backcast as on the forward cast.

The reason for this unusual action is in the nature of the weight we cast. In fly casting the weight is in the flexible fly line, not in the lure, as is the case with spinning or bait casting. When spinning or bait casting, the weight is contained within a few inches and the cast is easy on the back swing and forceful on the forward cast. To cast a fly, the long, flexible weight of the fly line (measured in feet) must be completely unrolled behind you before you begin the forward stroke. The essentially weightless fly is carried along, almost like a passenger, to reach its destination. A second difference is that, unlike spinning and bait casting lures, the heavier a fly is, the more difficult it is to cast!

Have you ever thrown anything backward? More than once? This is the challenge! No one of us, on the first attempt to fly cast, has any arm muscles already trained to throw backward. It will take practice, and is the reason why fly casting is a bit more difficult to learn than other types of casting. On the other hand, just think, if it weren't for fly casting you might go all through life having wasted that backward-throwing-muscle potential, just as we waste much of the potential of our left hand and arm if we are right handed, or vice versa.

As I think about what might simulate a backcast so that you can understand it, I can only come up with a marshmallow that has been toasted over an open fire on the end of a supple stick or twig. You can flip it backward off the stick, over your shoulder, for twenty or thirty feet. The next time you find yourself holding a pencil, a long-handled cooking spoon, or anything that is basically a shaft, grip it with your thumb on top and pretend it is a twig bent downward with the weight of a toasted marshmallow on the end. Let your hand bend down with the weight of it.

Choose a target backcast spot on the wall behind you, above head level. Get the shaft moving carefully, then, with forearm and hand, *flip it* back and up, behind you. At the end of the flip there should be

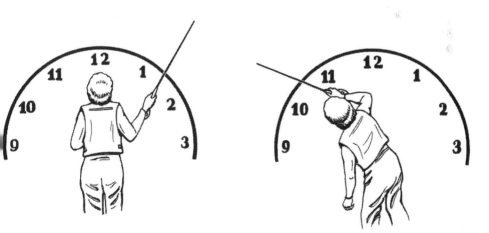

Elbow remains close to body on forehand casts (12 to 3); elbow lifts and body leans on backhand casts (12 to 9).

a 90-degree angle between your forearm and upper arm, and your wrist should be aligned with your forearm. This is the basic backcast movement.

Books on fly casting can be helpful but they are better as backups than as primary teachers. No matter how well written they are or how many illustrations they contain, it is difficult to learn a three-dimensional sport from the printed page. It is also almost impossible to analyze your own efforts. You'll save precious time and a lot of frustration by going to a school first and working with a book second.

Don't learn how to fly cast from someone with whom you are emotionally involved, unless that someone is an exception to the rule. When Lee and I were first married he wanted to teach me to fly his SuperCub. Because we loved each other I was sure we could do it, but more often than not, as the lessons came to a close, Lee was angry and I found myself close to tears. Someone else taught me to fly.

All the instructors I employ, and all those I know, think that women are better fly-casting students than are men. I agree, because most women start from zero. They do not expect anything magical to happen and progress one step at a time. Most men start from zero minus X; the minus X is what the instructor has to break down before they can start to progress. Men think they are expected to know how to do everything. Women don't. Perhaps in our liberation we, too, will pick up some of these masculine traits that we may be better off without.

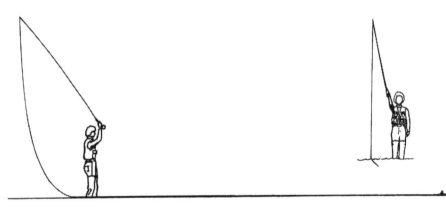

When obstacles prevent an aerial backcast, use a roll cast. Shown here are side and front views of set-up position. Keeping the fly on the water, lift the rod slowly and tilt it outward to belly line behind you. The forward stroke can roll line on or above the water for the presentation.

There are particular casting techniques to learn as your base: the roll cast, the basic pick-the-line-off-the-water-and-put-it-back-down cast, false casting, and shooting line. Learn them from both forehand and backhand positions. This group of casts makes you operational. When you have mastered them, learning the more complicated techniques, such as single and double hauls, will be quite easy.

The fly-casting stroke is a straight-line movement of the whole rod by the rod hand, in an acceleration to a stop. This means you start slowly, increase speed, and end abruptly. During the acceleration, the weight of the fly line bends the rod from the tip downward. This is called "loading" the rod. When the rod butt is stopped abruptly to end the acceleration, the rod "unloads." The limber tip, bent down with the line weight, flips from one side of the rod shaft to the other, and the long flexible line, continuing on its original path, passes over the tip and forms an open-ended unrolling loop.

Let me put that description into the set of fly-casting mechanics I have developed. Imagine that the fly line is on the water and the cast will include a backcast stroke and a forward cast stroke, ending with the line back on the water.

Part one of the backcast gets the rod, line, leader, and fly moving as a unit and is the *loading move*. Starting the stroke with the rod tip just above the water and without any slack in the line, lift the fly line to the line/leader connection to execute the loading move.

Part two continues and maximizes the loading action as the rod and line are accelerated with force to a sudden stop. The leader and fly are lifted out of the water with a *power snap* to end the stroke. The power snap encompasses the one instant of real force in the cast, and the rod, through the action of the arm, snaps from one position to another. The abrupt ending of the acceleration flips the fly line over the rod tip, from one side to the other, to form a new loop. To go back to the toasted marshmallow on the supple stick: getting it started slowly, so as not to lose it, is the loading move; flipping it off the stick is the power snap.

When the stroke is finished, the beginning of the new loop that has formed at the rod tip must then unroll completely behind you. Don't just wait while it unrolls; instead "follow through," moving your rod hand backward and upward a few inches. This backward follow-through is called *drift* and maintains the feeling of being connected to the fly line as it unrolls.

The forward stroke has the same two parts and follow-through. The loading move gets everything moving as a unit, the power snap projects the rod (and following line) toward the target area with a new

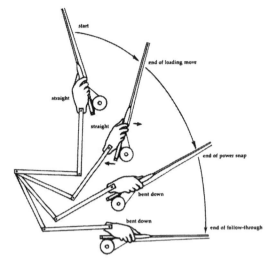

Forward cast

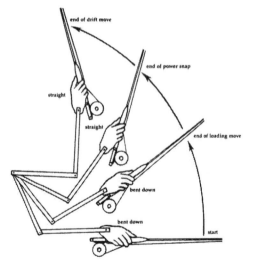

Backcast

Movement of the arm in the casting stroke. The forearm and upper arm move throughout the stroke, but the wrist/hand action is restricted to the power snap on both backcast and forward cast.

loop, and the arm and rod follow through (this time lowering) as the line unrolls above the water and then lands lightly.

Let's look at the parts of your arm and how they can work for you.

The Grip

Although you can fly cast with your forefinger on top of the grip, or even no fingers on top, the shortest route to proficiency is to use your thumb, in a flexed position, directly on top of the rod grip, in line with the shaft. There are limitations to the other grips but none with the thumb grip because this digit has its own muscle. If you learn to use it well, your fly line will always straighten out on the cast.

Align your hand and forearm so they rest *on top* of the rod grip and the reel seat is under your arm, not next to it.

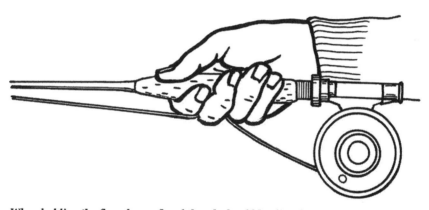

When holding the fly rod your flexed thumb should be directly on top of the grip and your forearm should rest on the reel seat.

Wrist and Hand Movement

Check to see how your wrist can be bent back, held straight, or bent down forward. Bending back is a *no-no*; it throws the rod tip and fly line downward, toward the water or low bushes you are always trying not to touch behind you. The wrist motion to use is the small movement encompassed between *bent downward* and *straight*. It is such a small movement that you will surely think it isn't enough. The secret is that it is used with forearm movement (bending from the elbow), and then it is enough.

Small as the wrist movement is, you'll see its effects in the position of the rod grip relative to the underside of your wrist and forearm. Here are the visual clues: When the wrist is bent downward, notice that there is no open space between the grip and the underside of the forearm; when the wrist is straight, the grip will be at a 45-degree angle. If you have carelessly bent the wrist backward, that rod-to-forearm angle will enlarge to 90 degrees. Focus on these positions and angles to identify right and wrong wrist motion.

Elbow and Forearm Movement
Bending your elbow moves your forearm and hand back and up toward your upper arm. The longest strokes you'll make will bring your forearm muscle to your upper arm muscle. Then unbend your elbow and move the forearm forward. Combined with the wrist movement mentioned above you now have a back-and-forth movement of the forearm and hand, within which the hand and wrist move between bent-down and straight. It is a move within a move.

The wrist begins the backcast bent down in the loading move and

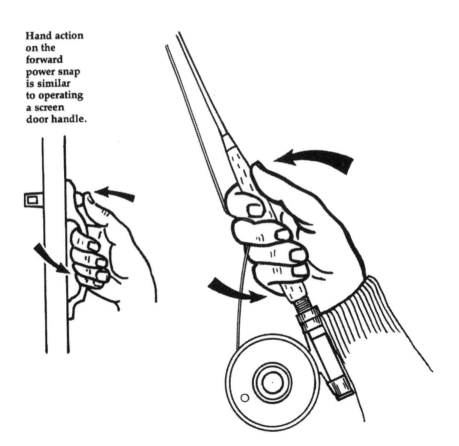

Hand action on the forward power snap is similar to operating a screen door handle.

flicks to straight on the power snap to end the backcast. It begins the forward cast in this straight position on the loading move and flicks to the bent-down position during the power snap to end the forward cast.

The flick from bent-down to straight on the backcast is a simple one along with the forearm moving backward too. The wrist flick forward is more complex. In getting from the straight wrist to the bent-forward wrist I compare the hand action to that required for a screen-door handle—one in which you push the round button with your thumb while you pull back with your other fingers to unlatch the door. To get a final and very helpful burst of speed out of the rod tip at the end of the forward cast, pretend you're opening a screen door, pushing the rod shaft forward with your thumb toward the target while you use your last two fingers to pull the rod handle back up against your wrist. This precise hand action is one of the secrets to being a better-than-average caster because it enhances line control.

Shoulder and Upper Arm Movement
Think about running without using your hip joints. Your thighs would hang down and you would kick your feet up backward from the knees in order to propel your body forward. To run smoothly we need to use our whole leg, from foot to hip joint. In fly casting you need to use the whole arm for the same reasons. So, to the back-and-forth motion of the forearm and hand we add the up-and-down motion of the whole arm. This movement comes from the shoulder joint.

Once you incorporate the up-and-down shoulder movement, you won't have to move your forearm back and forth as much. End the upward backcast with your hand above eye level and with a 90-degree angle between your forearm and upper arm. Keep that angle as you begin the forward cast and then project the forearm and hand forward, just a few degrees to finish the cast, ending with a still-bent arm.

Body Motion
Participants in all sports use body motion to stay aligned with the target and to smoothly apply any needed force. While all anglers benefit from body motion, it is extremely valuable for shorter women. Short women have short arms; long casts require long strokes. When you run out of arm length, you can increase the speed of your stroke to help, but body motion can actually increase your stroke length.

Drop back the foot on your casting side. Shift your weight to the back foot on the backcast, and to the forward foot on the forward cast. Simple. This body motion will do two things for you: It will add many

Shifting your weight during the cast increases the length of your stroke and makes the application of power more fluid.

inches to the length of your stroke (it adds twelve to fourteen inches to mine) and help relax you, thereby smoothing out your casting effort.

The overall casting stroke has been described as an acceleration to a stop. To stop at the peak requires hand strength. Compress all of your hand and arm muscles in what you might term a "death clutch," squeezing the cork grip of the rod to stop it in place. Follow the squeeze with immediate relaxation and a follow-through backward while the line unrolls. Then slowly begin the acceleration again, ending with another fast clutch and another relaxing follow-through.

So there are two clutches, two instants in which your strength is brought to bear: one on the backcast and one on the forward cast. The act of casting will develop your hand and forearm muscles, but you can work out with small dumbell weights to build your strength more quickly.

The difference between good casters and mediocre ones lies in little details, and in the disciplines needed to maintain control over the line. There are certain factors that take away your control. One is using your wrist instead of your elbow as the primary pivot; another is swinging the arm outward from the shoulder instead of keeping the elbow forward of the shoulder in the plane of the cast. Styles that include these factors can work at short distances, but you'll run into trouble with long casts or during difficult wind conditions. In addition to learning a general style that will give you unlimited potential, there are basic disciplines that will ensure almost every cast will be good, maybe even perfect.

Backcast Details and Disciplines

1. Start the backcast with the rod against the underside of your forearm.

2. When taking line off the water, start the pickup with the rod tip low to the water and with no slack in the line.

3. On the pickup, end the backcast stroke as the fly comes out of the water.

4. End all backcast strokes with the rod hand in front of, above, or in line with your shoulder, but not behind it.

5. Keep your elbow forward of your shoulder regardless of the angle of the cast.

6. Use a squeeze stop on the backcast, with a straight but not stiff wrist.

Forward Cast Details and Disciplines

1. On every cast, *aim* at a particular inch of water.

2. Determine a hand-to-target line before beginning the forward cast. Make a straight-line path along it, leading with the elbow and finishing with the hand.

3. Use enough acceleration to completely unroll the line above the water (unless you consciously choose to do otherwise).

4. Use hand and wrist action in the forward cast power snap by pushing forward with your thumb as far as you can and using your last two fingers to pull the rod grip back up against your forearm.

Overall Details and Disciplines

1. As the line lengthens use body motion, as it is needed, to lengthen the casting stroke.

2. With weight-forward or triangle-taper lines, never pick up more line than the total weighted section.

3. Mark your line at the end of the weighted section on weight-forward lines to facilitate this maximum length pickup. (A waterproof marker pen works well.)

4. Keep slack from forming between the line hand and the first guide on the rod during the cast by moving both hands along parallel lines.

5. Watch and analyze the way in which the line unrolls on every forward cast.

To be good at any sport or to develop a skill, you must practice. Fly-O, the indoor practice rod, is available from your fly tackle dealer and can do wonders for you in five-minute segments a couple of times a week. It is limited to rod-hand use, because the yarn doesn't slide through the guides, but the rod hand is the important hand, the one that controls the cast. Practice basic casts with Fly-O, always aiming at a target. Use a book on the floor, the buttons on the sofa cushions, the finial on a lamp shade, or anything suitable that will develop your eye-hand-target coordination.

Outdoors, with your trout tackle and a piece of yarn on the leader to simulate a fly, aim at targets like the individual leaves of bushes, the slightly opened garage door, the hubcaps or headlights on your car, or a partially opened window. Once you start looking, targets are easy to find and they can turn repetitive practice into sessions that are both challenging and fun.

6

The Trout

The trout, because he is a right dainty fish and also a right fervent biter, we shall speak next of him. He is in season from March until Michaelmas. He is in clean gravel bottom and in a stream. You can angle for him at all times with a lying or running ground-line, except in leaping time and then with an artificial fly; and early with a running ground-line, and later in the day with a float-line. You must angle for him in March with a minnow hung on your hook by the lower nose, without float or sinker, drawing it up and down in the stream till you feel him hooked. In the same time, angle for him with a ground-line with an earthworm, as the surest bait. In April, take the same baits, and also the lamprey, otherwise called "seven eyes," also the cankerworm that grows in a great tree, and the red snail. In May, take the stone fly and the grubworm under the cow turd, and the silkworm, and the bait that grows on a fern leaf. . . . In August, take a flesh fly and the big red worm and the fat of bacon, and bind them about your hook. In September, take the earthworm and the minnow. In October, take the same,

for they are special for the trout at all times of the year.
From April to September the trout leaps; then angle for him
with an artificial fly appropriate to the month. These flies
you will find at the end of this treatise, and the months
with them.

In Juliana's time little or nothing was known about the aquatic insects of the trout streams; the angler's interest in stream entomology started to develop in the late nineteenth century. All of her suggested baits are from the land and fall into the category of "terrestrials," except for the minnows.

The best trout anglers I know are those who started fishing with live bait. If it is possible, I hope you will at some time fish with a worm or minnow *"special for trout at all times of the year"* on your fly rod. Women have a sensitivity that is helpful in bait fishing, so you can expect to be successful. The line in your hand will act as a telegraph system. You'll get subtle messages as the trout picks up the bait softly and perhaps repositions it before swallowing. A tightening of all that lies between you should trigger your strike. Success with live bait will deepen your understanding of the trout as a wild creature and add to your expertise in using artificials.

If it is not in your nature to fish with live bait, try a minnow-imitating streamer, which is one of the surest ways to catch trout. Streamers are always a good backup fly to carry along with your selection of aquatic insect imitations. (Earthworm imitations have yet to be accepted in the fly category.)

For more than any other reason, I love trout fishing because of where trout live. Their home is in clean and flowing water, water that gathers oxygen as it grows from tiny snow-melt trickles and puddles in the higher elevations of the watershed to become small brooks and creeks, which then empty into streams and rivers. The tributaries remain as spawning and nursery areas and often provide the relief of cooler water during the hot summer months. With the addition of abundant insect life, trout have all they need to flourish.

Abundant insect life is also found in the West's "spring creeks," which arise from springs. A constant flow of pure, clean water and a nearly constant temperature provide predictable and generous hatches that make these often weed-laden creeks and their selective trout particularly challenging to trout fishermen.

Trout are, in a stream's chain of life, both predator and prey. Hatching from eggs in late winter, they absorb their sustaining yolk sacks in roughly five weeks; then the little fry must find food, as free-swimming fish, in shallow water. Tiny as they are, their food must be even tinier, and the larvae of midges fills the bill for the little predators. In three or four months the fry are still only 3 or 4 inches long, but they are able to ingest increasingly larger insects. As they grow they move from the shallows into the stream's main flow and, at maturity, into the best feeding lies. Starting at birth, and for all of their lives, trout are prey for other fish (including their own species), animals of the streams and shores such as otters and mink, and, of course, kingfishers, herons, and other birds. This is why a fleeting shadow on the water can send a trout scurrying for cover.

With no hands to satisfy their curiosity, trout must take into their mouths anything that interests them. Imagine the bits and pieces of wood, leaves, and grass that go into those mouths and are ejected as the trout discerns between what is good to eat and what isn't. Life being what it is, nothing is ever known completely, and so the trout's mistakes and remaining curiosity—along with his role as a predator— are factors that play in favor of the angler.

There are four common species of trout, each with its own distinct personality: brook, rainbow, brown, and cutthroat.

Brook trout, *Salvelinus fontinalis*, are actually chars and are native to northeastern North America. Distinguishing marks are yellow spots, red spots within blue circles, wavy lines (vermiculations) on their backs, and the dead-give-away white edges on their lower, pink-red fins.

I think of brook trout as impetuous kids or teenagers; they're playful. They seem to be attracted to anything that is red or brightly colored and are more easily tricked into taking a fly than the other species. They make up for their lack of sophistication with style, often leaping completely out of the water to take the fly on the way down. A

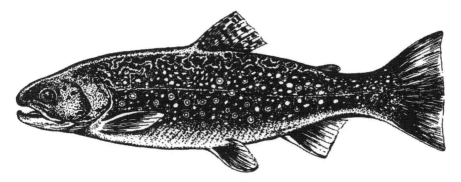

Brook trout

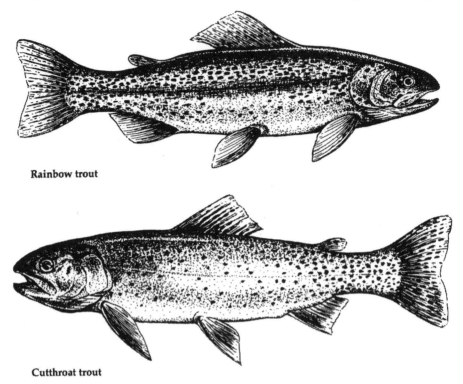

Rainbow trout

Cutthroat trout

6-inch brookie once took my fly in such a way on an otherwise fishless morning (it was a #12 Royal Wulff, almost as big as he was) and raised my spirits for the day. Although I have caught brook trout weighing up to 4 pounds in Labrador, I always think of that spunky little fellow on the Ashuelot River in New Hampshire when I hear the words "brook trout."

Rainbow trout, *Oncorhynchus mykiss*, are another native American, but from the Pacific slopes. They have a pinkish red lateral stripe that is especially noticeable in adult fish. There are dark spots on the body, upper fins, and tail. The great game-fish steelhead is a sea-run rainbow.

Rainbows are like young adults, sophisticated but not too much so. Flashy in appearance, adaptable to most American streams, the rainbow is the species most available to the angling public through stocking programs. When hooked, its acrobatic jumps are a joy to behold. I once hooked a 16-inch wild rainbow in the Delaware River near Hancock, New York. It made my reel scream as it ran off all of my fly line and twenty yards of the backing line, making it comparable to a small Atlantic salmon. A stocked fish could never have given me that thrilling experience.

Cutthroat trout, *Oncorhynchus clarki*, are native to the Rockies and the West Coast. Cutthroat, true to their name, have a distinctive red slash under their gill covers. Their body is yellowish green and has dark spots, which are most heavily concentrated toward the tail. Many anglers feel that "cutts" lack challenge, which may be why they seem like comfortable friends and relatives. They can be predictable. Nevertheless, I have found them to be very challenging when they are taking midges in spring creeks, and any fisherman who passes through Yellowstone Park usually looks forward to offering a #18, or smaller, "Hank of Hair" fly to the cutthroat in Buffalo Ford.

Brown trout, *Salmo trutta*, are native to Europe, but they were successfully introduced to this continent in the 1880s. A yellowish brown base color, they boast dark brown or black spots on the upper body with some red or orange ones in the lateral line area. A deep-bodied 13- to 15-inch wild brown is my idea of a gorgeous trout.

The most mature and wary trout, browns are the wise adults of the trout population. The biggest ones are usually caught at night. Because they have been fished over for several centuries, browns have the built-in wisdom that contact with humans eventually develops in all creatures. When you fool a good brown trout into taking your fly, you feel as if you've really measured up to a challenge. Although they

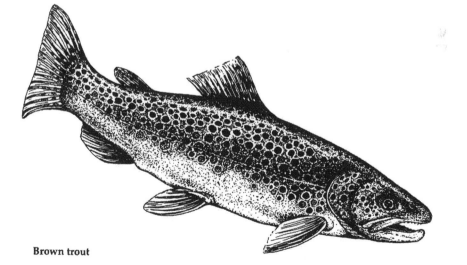

Brown trout

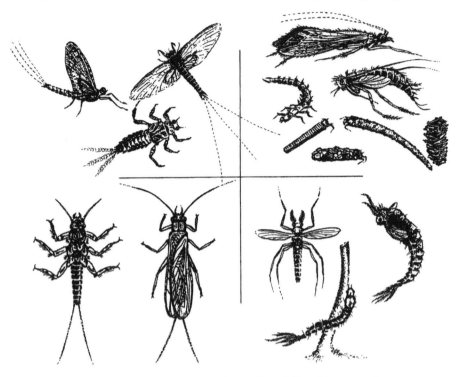

Aquatic insects. Clockwise from top left: mayfly, caddis, midge, stonefly.

occasionally leap like rainbows, browns fight with more tricks up their sleeves than the other species and require more strategy from the angler.

There are three stages in a fisherman's life: First you'll want to catch as many fish as possible; in the second stage you'll want to catch the biggest; and finally, you'll care only about the most difficult fish. You can be at different angling stages with each species of trout or, in the bigger picture, with different species of fish.

Trout fishing is the most complex of all fly fishing in the challenges it offers. It can keep you intellectually stimulated for the rest of your life. The range, in physical size and variety, of food available in the trout's world, and the understanding of all the life cycles involved, is mind-boggling.

Fortunately, the character of the fish itself makes it unnecessary for you to boggle your mind. Trout are low on the intelligence scale, not even as smart as your house pet, although one trout can be smarter than another and they learn from experience. They are competitive, playful, and wary individuals. They also know nothing about hooks, or the steelmills that make them.

A trout's needs are simple: safety, food, and comfort. Trout seek safety in deep water and look for obstructions under which they can hide. On a stream bottom, debris of all sizes and shapes offers good hiding places. Natural characteristics of the stream, such as undercut banks, overhanging grasses, weed beds, tree roots, and rock ledges, also provide a haven. Whenever danger threatens, trout move swiftly to their favorite safe spot, a place they know well and can count on.

The trout's food consists mainly of four groups of aquatic insects: mayflies, caddisflies, stoneflies, and midges in all their forms—larva, nymph or pupa, and adult. Noninsects such as snails, crayfish, salamanders, minnows, and fry are prey, too. Additionally, there are land-based foods that find their way into the water. Known as terrestrials, they include ants, grasshoppers, beetles, leaf hoppers, and all the worms and grubs and caterpillars that Dame Juliana listed. Trout will eat anything that moves if it is accessible.

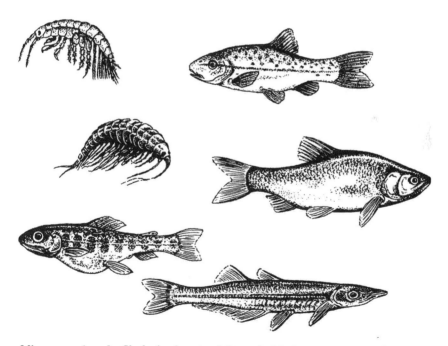

Minnows and scuds. Clockwise from top left: scuds, black-nosed dace, red shiner, brook silverside, brook trout fry.

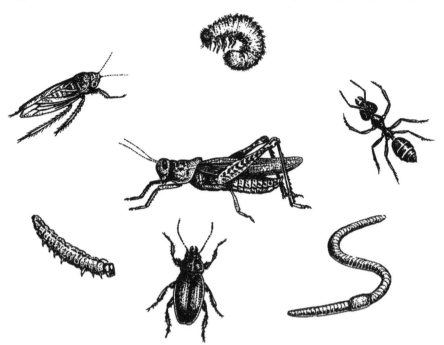

Terrestrials. Clockwise from top left: leaf hopper (0.1"), grub (0.5"), ant (0.4"), worm (3"), beetle (0.8"), caterpillar (1.5"), grasshopper (center—1.8").

Trout find comfort in the speed of the water's flow, in the oxygen content, and in the temperature. A trout may choose a different place to lie when he is resting than when he is feeding, but each will suit his purpose so that he does not expend too much energy for the rewards. He will feed on the edges of currents rather than in the current, and when he rests, he'll choose slower water.

Rapid water, water with some turbulence, creates the oxygen that trout need. Incidentally, it is free oxygen—as in air—not the chemical type that is part of the compound H_2O, water. Heat removes the free oxygen from the water and, therefore, temperature is a very important factor in where a trout will be found during hot weather and low water conditions. Remember that trout are cold-blooded; their bodies take on the temperature of the water that surrounds them.

The cold (33 to 45 degrees Fahrenheit) water of winter and early spring makes trout sluggish so they won't chase food, whether they're eating nymphs on the bottom or taking midges on the surface. You'll have to put your imitation right in its mouth. As the water warms to 45 to 54 degrees, trout move around more easily, their digestion speeds up, and they are more likely to catch the insect larvae and pupae, or your imitations of them. At 54 to 66 degrees you've got the best of it: Not only will the fully active trout chase insects or your underwater imitations, but they will also rise freely to dry flies in these warmer water temperatures.

A stream thermometer can provide the magic answer to the question, How close to the trout do my presentations have to be today?

Once the water's temperature reaches the 70s a dangerous period ensues. As the water's oxygen content diminishes, the trout leave their normal lies to find springs or travel upstream to tributaries or their mouths, where cooler, oxygenated water is spilled into the main stream. An unknowing angler can cast her heart out in barren water if she isn't tuned in to the importance of water temperature.

Safety, food, and comfort determine where trout will lie. Recognizing the water in which trout lie to feed requires that you learn to "read" water. Reading water and proper fly presentation are the two most important factors in becoming a successful trout angler.

A trout's resting lie (A) often provides him a hiding place. His feeding lie (B) is close to the food-bringing main current.

7

Reading Water

*Here I will declare in what place of the water you must
angle. . . . in a river you must angle in every place where it
is deep and clear at the bottom, as in gravel or clay without
mud or weeds, and especially if there is a kind of whirling of
water or a covert—such as a hollow bank or great roots of
trees or long weeds floating above in the water—where the
fish can . . . hide themselves at certain times. . . . Also . . .
in deep, swift streams, and also in waterfalls and weirs,
floodgates and millraces . . . and where the water rests by
the bank and where the current runs close by and it is deep
and clear at the bottom; and in any other places where you
can see any fish rise or do any feeding.*

Juliana's description is a good start on the subject of where trout
are to be found within clean and flowing water, taking into account its
needs for food, comfort, and safety.

Understanding hydraulics, the science of flowing water, is one of
the more masculine facets of fly fishing. Boys and young men seem to

take to it like ducks take to water, but few of the women I know come by it naturally. Perhaps the freedom boys have to explore the physical aspects of the world around them, while girls have traditionally been more sheltered, is at the root of this ability. When I first looked at a trout stream and saw the beautiful patterns created by the different currents and obstructions, they had no meaning to me—just as I thought trout swam haphazardly through the water. Even today, on water that is unfamiliar to me, it takes longer for me than my expert companions to read all that is there. Trout fishing is not a competition, however, so a little more time is mine for the taking and I eventually figure it out. You will too.

Remember the simple fact that water runs downhill. A river or stream's volume changes in depth and speed as a result of the shape of the streambed and the amount of drop in elevation. The character of the streambed, which includes mud, clay, bedrock, gravel of various sizes, boulders, and debris from tree-lined banks, creates areas within the water that vary the speed and direction of the flow. Obstructions to the water's flow create quiet places for the trout to rest or feed.

Water doesn't move at the same speed at all levels, even if it is unobstructed. It moves fastest a few inches below the surface, then slows down gradually to a less hurried speed at the bottom. Stronger flows can dig into areas of streambed that cannot withstand its pressure to form depressions and undercut banks. Both depressions in the streambed and undercut banks offer good resting and/or feeding places for trout.

The areas of different character in the stream have common names: pools, eddies, runs, pocket water, riffles, edges or seams, and gravel bars.

A pool is like a basin or bathtub. It has a head, where the water enters through a narrower space, and a tail, below which the stream's character again changes. Near the head of the pool, trout generally lie to one side or the other of the current or beneath it, where it has slowed down, to easily feed on the insect delights of the moveable feast. You'll find trout at the pool's tail where the flow narrows, as does the spread of food. As Dame Juliana observed, the bottoms of deep pools also serve as safe resting places for bigger fish. Think of a pool as a fish hotel; some guests are eating while others are resting out of sight.

Eddies, or backwaters, are surprising places. Lee calls them the garbage cans of the streams. An eddy is an area of sometimes circular motion in which the current moves opposite to the flow of the main stream. Debris and insects tend to accumulate in the large, circular

eading Water

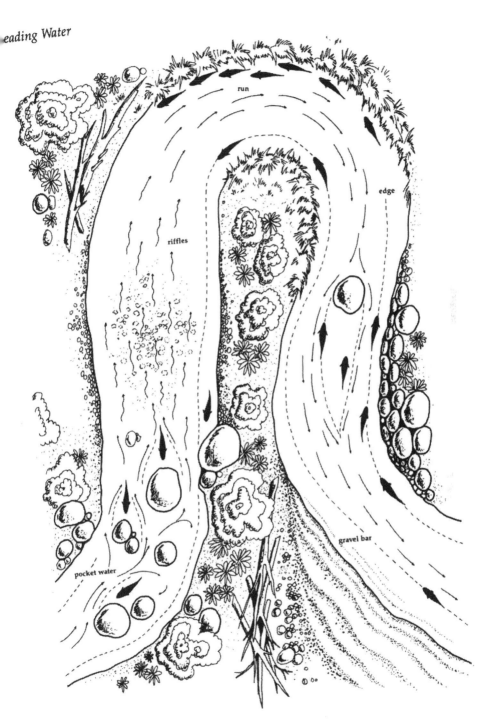

eddies, and the heavier-than-water particles will eventually reach the slow-moving center of the eddy and drop out. If you have ever noticed a trout, which supposedly always faces upstream, comfortably facing downstream, you've seen one in an eddy. Trout lie with their noses into the current—whether or not it is literally upstream—to breathe the life-giving flow of water through their gills. Eddies are particularly attractive to trout during flood conditions or in the spring when the water is high and cold and the main flow is faster than normal. Then the trout are cold, too, and not as active and strong as they will be in warmer water.

Eddies can also be quiet places formed by anything that interrupts the water's flow. They can be visible on the surface or invisible and closer to the streambed. Rocks, logs, debris, even your wader-clad legs can form an eddy in a current and attract trout.

A run is a steady flow of water that is relatively smooth, yet deep enough to provide safety and comfort for trout. While most trout streams contain runs, it's the type of water flow seen most frequently in meadow streams. As the stream meanders it tends to undercut banks on the outside of the curves where the flow is fastest and create shallows on the inside of the curves where the flow is considerably slower. Trout tend to lie on the deep side in the runs against the undercut banks.

Pocket water is a stream section with exposed rocks, islands, weedbeds, or other obstructions. Pockets are small areas behind and between the obstructions that will often hold trout. The best pockets have depth, to provide safety, and an easily accessible flow of food.

Riffles are relatively broad and shallow areas of swift water running over rough or gravelly streambed. They give insects places to grow and hide. Trout won't spend much time in riffles during the day if they feel vulnerable, choosing instead to feed there under the cover of darkness. There are exceptions, such as when the hatch is heavy and the trout are hungry. During such circumstances, riffles can be real hot spots.

Edges or seams are the lines formed where the central flow of water, such as in a pool or run, slides alongside slower water at the stream's shallower edges. Trout lie just inside the slower water and move into the faster water to take advantage of food carried by the current.

Gravel bars are the result of seasonal changes in the level of the river. Gravel can range in size from pebbles to boulders. Ice jams and high water can gouge the bottom and release gravel so it moves downriver and piles up in ridges. The bars thus formed are often exposed during low water. In normal or high water they are good fishing areas because they provide habitat for insects, crawfish, darters, and so on, as well as serving as pathways for the angler to or through the deeper water.

It is easy to recognize the characteristics of areas in small to medium-size streams, but they exist in broad rivers, too. These are more difficult to discern, but knowing they are probably there will help you find them. For example, if you put your eyes at the level of the water's surface, you will see a slight depression if there is a "bath-tub" on the bottom. Broken water on the surface can reflect relatively deep boulders that will have pockets and/or eddies behind them.

What you are looking for is a particular speed of water flow that will satisfy the trout's needs for feeding. This is thought to be a flow of from one to two miles per hour, on or beneath the surface. Another reference is a flow of one foot per second.

After years of using words to identify this ideal condition to our fishing school students, Lee, who is a pilot, suddenly realized that if a wind sock could show him the speed and direction of the flow of air necessary for safe landings, then a "water sock" could give the same

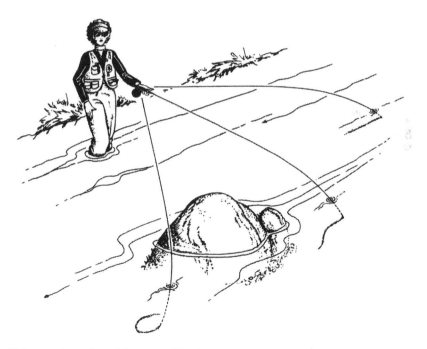

Using a water sock enables you to identify possible trout lies.

information about the flow of water, at various levels and relative to obstructions, for the best lies for trout.

Make an instant water sock by attaching a one-foot-long piece of brightly colored yarn to your rod tip. Carry it in your vest and fish a pool on your favorite river. Take note of any spot in the pool where you see a rise, catch a fish, or see any other sign of a trout's being there. When you have finished fishing, tie on the yarn and go to each of those places. Dip your rod tip into the water where the trout was to see the effect of the flow on your water sock. Then look at the surface for signs of how to identify this ideal speed. Now use this knowledge to explore the rest of the pool to learn the differences between the surface signs of good and bad lies.

The water sock will indicate the velocity and direction of the flow. Move around the pool from one side to the other and down through to the tail, dipping the yarn behind rocks, moving it slowly from top to bottom in the deepest areas, and letting it identify eddies. Put it in any place that interests you. You will see a change in the yarn's behavior with each new circumstance. When you have gone all the way through the pool you'll have a "data base" to which you can add by using your water sock in other kinds of water such as pocket water, riffles, runs, and seams. The hands-on experience will be more valuable than all of the descriptions of perfect water flow you'll ever read and, at the very least, it will make what you read more understandable.

8

Approach and Presentation

*And for the first and principal point of angling, always keep
yourself away from the water, from the sight of the fish,
either far back on the land or else behind a bush, so that the
fish may not see you. For if they do, they will not bite. Also
take care that you do not shadow the water any more than
you can help, for that is a thing which will soon frighten
the fish. And if a fish is frightened, he will not bite for a
long time afterward.*

In the fifteenth century, dear Juliana's line of horsehair was probably tied to the tip of her rod and, without a reel, the maximum length
of her cast was predetermined. She could never present her bait, or a
fly, at the distances we can, so the chances of frightening fish gave her
cause for much concern. In the twentieth century we must follow the
same rules, but our tackle gives us the latitude to remain at a safe
distance.

The vision of trout is quite different from ours. If you visualize a
clock with a fish's nose pointing toward 12, the right eye sees from

about 11 to 4 o'clock and the left eye sees from 8 to 1 o'clock. This is its monocular vision. The two fields overlap ahead (leaving a blind spot directly ahead of its nose) from about 11 o'clock to 1 o'clock; in this region the trout has binocular vision. A trout may first see your fly with one eye or the other but he will turn to see it with both eyes before intercepting it.

It is possible to catch a trout even when you are visible to each other. The determining factors are the trout's distance from what he regards as safety (deep water, a big rock, the protective roots of a tree) and his distance from you. Obviously wild creatures can be frightened, but they do not live fearfully. They have an invisible zone of safety around them, which includes the distance at which they will stop feeding without bolting. At that distance you could be a one-alarm danger. When you get any closer it is two-alarm danger and they are gone.

Whether or not you can see a trout in the stream, move toward your casting position slowly and carefully. Then stand still for a while before beginning to cast. When you remain motionless, in the stream or on the bank, in time you become another piece of the scenery. In Yellowstone Park's Buffalo Ford, it is common for anglers to have cutthroats come and lie in the eddy formed by their legs when they have stood in one place for five or ten minutes. Buffalo Ford is heavily fished and the trout have become as used to anglers as they have to the resident elk and buffalo. In truly wild areas, where anglers are scarce, the trout will be much more wary.

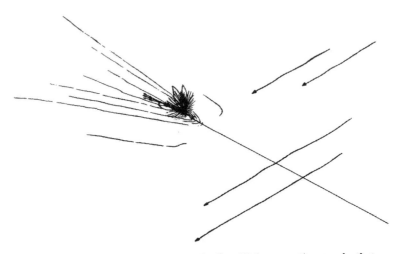

When the leader tippet is under tension, the fly will drag, creating a wake that indicates the fly is attached to something.

The traditional patterns of presentation are designed to approach the trout in a nonalarming manner. Flies are presented in one of two ways: *under tension*, with line, leader, and fly at full extension from the rod tip, or *free floating*, in which the fly drifts freely with the current. With free-floating flies, slack leader near the fly is desirable but all other slack should be kept to a minimum. Drag on the fly must be avoided, unless you make a conscious decision to let it occur.

Drag indicates that the fly is not drifting freely with the current; that the fly is, in fact, attached to something. The final tippet, when straightened out and under tension because of its position on the water relative to the current, will drag the fly in a way that is unnatural for a free-drifting creature. The tension can start when an intervening current bellies either the fly line or the main body of the leader. Regardless of where tension begins, it will travel continuously until it reaches the fly and "puts drag on it."

Under Tension

Making your cast diagonally, down and across the stream, allows the fly to be captured by the current and appear alive as it moves under tension back across the stream to your side. This is the traditional pattern for fishing wet flies and streamers, but you can fish nymphs this way, too. Using this method to "cover" water will put your fly within sight of every fish within your casting range. It is an ideal technique for exploring an unfamiliar section of water because you can observe conditions and fish at the same time.

There are several steps to what anglers call covering water. On your first cast put the fly a few feet inside the current, diagonally downstream. Put the fly line under a finger of your rod hand and keep the rod tip pointed toward the fly as it moves across the current. When it stops "swimming" at the edge of the current below you, the presentation is complete.

Next, strip line off your reel in an amount you will duplicate on each of the following casts, such as two or three feet. Make the second cast in the same direction and at the same angle as the first, shooting the additional amount of line. From the same spot, continue adding the measured amount of line on each cast until you have reached your casting limit, or the far side of the current.

With this now final length, you will continue to cover water by taking a step downstream between casts for the same distance each time (for example, your chosen two or three feet) until your fly has been fished through all the water you think may hold trout.

In this downstream and underwater presentation, always watch your fly or where you think it is. Because the fly can move pretty fast

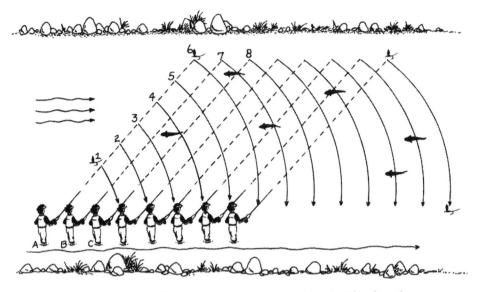

To cover water with wet flies or streamers, begin at position A and make a short cast diagonally downstream. The fly will float through an arc of water indicated by the solid line. Make your casts progressively longer until you've covered all the water you can from that position (6). Keep this line length and move downstream a few feet before each cast (7, 8, and so on).

in this technique, a trout might not be able to catch it. If you see a trout flash at the fly but there is no connection, duplicate the cast but try to slow it down.

You can slow the speed of the fly's movement in one of two ways. The first is to lower your rod to a position just above the surface while the fly is traveling across the stream, or lower it suddenly at a particular spot. The second and more effective technique is to *mend line* against the current. Without altering the path of the fly, make a half-circle lifting motion with your fly rod to move the main portion of the fly line back toward the current's flow. If you are on the left side of the current, its force on your line is from the right. You would mend to the right to slow the speed of the fly. Mending is a line-handling technique that you can use with all presentations.

Within this quartering downstream technique, you can vary the action of the fly. If you do nothing, it will swim steadily across the current. Your choices in adding variety are through rod action, stripping action or both at the same time. You can bounce the rod tip up and down to take the fly's motion out of the "steady" category; you can strip in (retrieve) line by pulling it from behind your rod hand's middle finger, in various lengths, to give the fly a darting action.

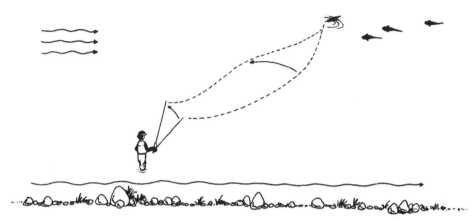

Mending line against the current with wet flies and streamers to slow down your fly. Make a half-circle lifting motion with the rod, in the upstream direction, almost like flipping one end of a jump rope. Don't move the fly.

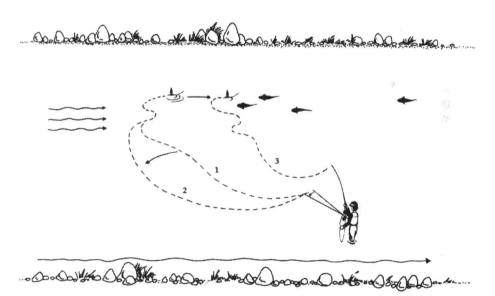

Mending line with a dry fly. If intervening currents put drag on the fly before it can reach the trout, mend the belly of the line upstream as early in the presentation as can be done effectively.

Realize that you are shortening the line with the stripping action, which will change how you cover the water.

With this method of presentation the fly moves under tension at all times, so a strike will be felt whether it is seen or not, and the fish usually hooks itself.

If the effects of stream flow on a fly are a mystery to you, it might be helpful to perform the following exercise. Put a large, brightly colored fly on your leader and, at various line lengths that keep it visible to you, try different retrieves and speeds and mending of the line. You'll be able to see how these affect the fly as it moves across the current. What you learn with a visible fly will help you to be more effective with one that is invisible.

Free Floating

Casting upstream is the traditional way to fish dry flies and un-weighted nymphs. The dries, of course, then float downstream on the surface or in the surface film, and the nymphs float below the surface. If they do not float freely, but instead move under some tension, drag is created and your attempt at deception may be discovered by the trout. The construction of your leader, your casting technique, and the ability to mend line are all important parts of success with free-floating flies.

Presenting a fly upstream keeps you out of the trout's vision. Exactly where you position yourself below the trout is important, however. A cast made directly upstream of the angler may put the fly line and/or leader directly over the fish's back and "put him down," so a better presentation position is below the area you wish to fish but from across the stream. Hence, "quartering" upstream.

Make the cast as accurately and delicately as you can to place the fly exactly where you want it. Put the fly line under your rod hand's middle finger. As the fly drifts downstream, keep your eye on the artificial and on the little circle of water around it. At the same time, follow the fly line with your rod tip, using your peripheral vision to keep it in view, and retrieve any slack line as it is formed. (You'll be busy!) The length of the effective float will be ended by drag, which can sometimes take your fly beneath the surface.

Watching the fly will let you see the first sign of drag on it, or, better yet, you'll see the nose or mouth of a trout that precedes the fly's disappearance! The strike here is visual. You are not going to be sent a tugging message. The trout will take in the fly, recognize the deception, and eject it all in the blink of an eye. It's that fast; after all, he's been practicing all of his life.

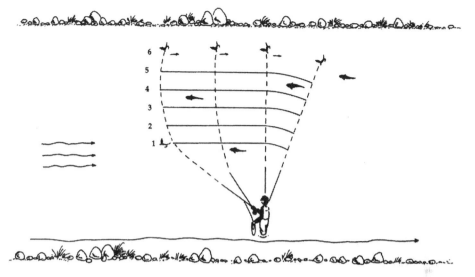

A cast quartering upstream enables you to drift a dry fly naturally with the current. At the end of the straight-line drift, pick up the fly. To cover the water, when trout are not rising, start with short casts and lengthen them across the stream. Then move upstream and cover a new section.

Unless I only have to move the line closest to the rod tip, I find it difficult to mend line with dry flies without moving the fly. So, if the intervening currents are going to make the presentation difficult, I change my position relative to the target area by moving up to be a little more directly across the stream. Then I use the *reach cast*.

This technique entails casting to the target area so that the line, leader, and fly will unroll above the water. After you've made the stroke, and before the line and fly actually land on the water (this is follow-through time), "reach" upstream with a swing of your whole arm and whole rod, "slipping," or releasing, extra line so your accuracy will be maintained and the fly will not fall short of the target. The bulk of the fly line and leader should land upstream of the fly and delay the onset of drag.

Another way to combat drag in tough conditions is to use long leader tippets that can't quite straighten out and so land with slack in them. Any slack that you can induce next to the fly usually can give you the time needed to drift it effectively.

In some circumstances, you may want to extend an upstream drift into a downstream drift. As the fly drifts below where you stand, pull

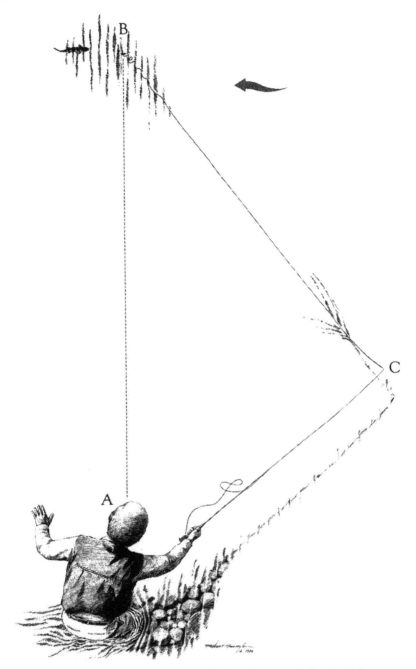

Reach cast. The cast is made (A–B) to unroll above the water. Before touchdown, arm and rod "reach" upstream (to C) as line hand releases slack. The resulting configuration delays drag on the fly.

extra line from the reel and stroke the rod gently from side to side, releasing line at the same time to slide through the rod's guides. Don't let the stroking movement affect the leader and fly.

When you see a fish feeding, check for a rhythmic pattern to his rises. If there is a great abundance of food moving toward him, you don't want your fly to get there just after he has taken a real insect. Time him. Then present the fly on what my friend Ed Van Put calls a "collision course with his mouth." While that is very descriptive, because I'm a mother I think of it as "spoon feeding."

Even the best anglers make a bad cast now and then. If you are casting to a rising trout and you goof up the cast, don't *snatch* it off the water in instant response. Your chances of catching that fish will go out the window. Instead, muzzle your emotions and let the line and fly drift right on through the area and make the next presentation a better one.

We all tend to take our fishing seriously and feel badly when we've "put a fish down" because of drag on a fly or a bad cast. After you've put the fish down, though, use the opportunity to experiment. Even if you think you won't catch a fish there today, meet the challenge and work that water until you *know how to do it*, for the next time! Chances are the trout will be there.

A dry fly or nymph presented in this quartering upstream pattern will cover only one strip of water, as opposed to the much greater coverage of the quartering downstream swing for wet flies and streamers, so we tend to fish this way only when we see trout working. Nevertheless, if you are fishing good water and its temperature is high enough to bring a trout to the surface, it may be worth covering with a dry fly. The technique then is to make the first drift in the closest likely place and then move increasingly farther across the stream on succeeding casts. Then move upriver a bit and start close again. In this way you won't disturb fish before you make the fly accessible to them.

These are the traditional fly-fishing techniques, the places where you begin. They are basic and they are always good. With experience and imagination, though, you can leave tradition. Try using a big, bushy dry fly downstream, under tension but on the surface, skating it across the current to tease trout into craziness in their attempt to catch it. You can also dead drift a dry fly downstream of you. Put slack into the line by aiming and unrolling the cast at a high angle and then lowering the rod tip quickly. You can cast an unweighted nymph quartering upstream, so that it dead drifts until it floats below your position, and then let it be caught by the current to move across it under tension.

Two flies on a leader, with one on a dropper, can be very effective,

In the weighted nymph presentation the rod is held high. Keep slack from forming in order to maintain contact with the bottom-drifting nymph.

too. A dropper is an 8- to 10-inch piece of monofilament that extends from the last leader knot before the fly. Use two wets, a wet and a nymph, or even a dry on the surface and a nymph or wet underneath. With two flies your casting must be done carefully. To avoid tangling the dropper, don't false cast to extend length, just pick up the line and put it back down, shooting a little line on each cast until you've reached the desired distance.

Nymph Fishing with Weight

Let me be clear on this: I hate fishing with weight in the fly or on the leader, but boy is it ever effective! Because trout feed year-round at the bottom of the stream, presenting your flies down there is devastatingly logical and effective. The fly itself can be weighted, or you can use split shot or wrap-around "lead matches" on your leader. If you do the latter, put the weight at the first knot above the fly.

I "hate" this method because the casting is neither easy nor beautiful. The lead weight changes everything. You must cast with less force and more slowly and, on the backcast, wait for the line, leader, and fly to be fully extended before coming forward. Leading the line through a circular or an oval pattern or changing planes between the backcast and the forward cast are other good techniques. Another casting alternative is a one-stroke cast. At the end of the fly's drift, lift the weight to the surface, then, turning upstream, reverse your forearm and hand so you can make a forward cast, accelerating very slowly.

For most anglers, weighted-nymph fishing is more difficult than wet- and dry-fly fishing. The challenge is part visual and part an extension of your sense of feeling. You have to be "in touch" at all times. The weighted nymph, like the dry fly, is dead drifting with the current along the streambed. This is essentially a short-line method. The basic system is to cast upstream, a few yards farther than the length of your short leader. It will take a few yards of moving with the flow for the fly to get down to the bottom. The rod tip is raised and slack is taken up so that your visual aid, the line and leader connection or a "strike indicator," is held on the surface or just under it and the leader and fly are directly below the visual aid. As the fly moves freely with the current, just above the bottom, everything is perfectly synchronized.

Relaxed concentration is the key. You won't feel the strike. When that synchronization is broken, when the current-related speed is interrupted, when everything *hesitates* for even a split second, there's your cue. Presume a trout has picked up the fly and strike!

Sometimes your fly will touch debris and give you a false alarm, but that's part of the game. It lets you know you are at the right depth. Anytime the leader hesitates, strike. If nothing interrupts the drift, the leader and line will eventually straighten to be under tension. Lift the nymph to the surface as if it were an emerging insect and you may draw a strike that way.

Once you have some experience with weighted nymphs, you'll be able to understand and try other techniques that you read about or see fellow anglers using.

With all the ways there are to present flies and all the flies of different character there are to present, there is no reason to ever be bored or to think that nothing will work. Perhaps nothing *will* work; fish are not always feeding, but don't think that way. Make each presentation as though you know a trout is waiting eagerly to take your fly.

9

Choosing the Right Fly

These are the twelve flies with which you must angle for the trout and grayling; and dub them just as you will now hear me tell.

March: The Dun Fly: The body of dun wool and the wings of the partridge. Another Dun Fly: the body of black wool; the wings of the blackest drake; and the jay under the wing and under the tail.

April: The Stone Fly

May: The Yellow Fly and the Black Leaper

June: The Dun Cut; the Maure Fly; the Tandy Fly

July: The Wasp Fly; the Shell Fly

August: The Drake Fly

John McDonald's *The Origins of Angling* tells us that in the centuries preceding the treatise, artificial flies were mentioned only once or twice in written references to the sport of fishing. Dame Juliana gave us the dressing for a dozen artificials that can be thought of as "the ancestors of the modern trout fly."

A dozen flies in 1496; thousands of fly patterns five hundred years later. Those first flies were wet flies. They had wings and were fished underwater. I wonder if Juliana thought of smearing them with mutton fat to make them float in the trout's "leaping time." Dry flies as we know them were not developed until the eighteenth century, so all of the fly patterns in those intervening centuries were wet-fly patterns. They caught fish, and still do, even though only the tiniest percentage of aquatic insects can be found alive underwater in the winged stage. Wet flies work because they move through the water, and movement in any medium indicates life.

Dry flies and nymphs, which are so popular today, are relatively young in their development because the science of entomology is young. As biologists have unraveled the mystery of the life cycles and identified the stages of the aquatic insects, the number of fly patterns has increased to include them. It is not necessary to have one of everything. Some patterns can be used to imitate several insects; what you must have, though, is something that will imitate each of the stages in a few sizes. With a magic marker and scissors, you can alter one of these if you encounter selective trout and don't have exactly what you think you need.

There are four important groups of aquatic insects that are easily identified in their adult stage. They are: mayflies, caddisflies, stoneflies, and midges. All spend 99 percent of their lives underwater and live only a day or two as air breathers for purposes of reproduction. It sounds like a fairy-tale scenario.

Mayflies

The mayfly's latin name, *Ephemeroptera*, translates roughly to "one day of adult life" plus "wing." When it is at rest on the water with its wings held upright, the mayfly looks like a little sloop.

More is known and has been written about the mayfly than any of the other aquatic insects, but it was Frank Sawyer's book *Keeper of the Stream* (1952, A & C Black, Great Britain) that focused my late-blooming attention on them. Frank was the riverkeeper of England's Upper Avon River. My husband, Lee, and I had the pleasure of spending part of a day with him, just visiting, in the late 1960s. I found him to be a gentle man with a passion for trout streams and for the creatures associated with them. Underlying the passion was a hard core of integrity. You believe what he says! How delighted I was to see how he says it in his book.

The life cycle of the mayfly. Clockwise from bottom left: nymph, emerger (center), dun, spinner, and spent spinner.

Speaking of big hatches of mayflies he had seen as a boy on the Upper Avon he writes: "I want to see (again) the sunlight glinting on a hundred thousand wings as the males dance in the meadows, and see the dipping and curtseying of the females as they sow the seed for a future generation. I want to see the whole surface of the river broken by the rises of excited trout—monsters brought to the surface by the temptation only a mayfly hatch can present, and the angler standing by me to be no less excited. For it seems to be that without the mayfly season there is a woeful gap in the charm of a river valley during mid-May to early June."

Mayflies are among the most beautiful and delicate creatures of the natural world; they seem almost to belong in an unnatural one. However, their very real bodies provide the bulk of the trout's food in the spring when the major hatches occur.

The life cycle for most of the major mayfly species lasts one year. Their eggs become nymphs that are categorized into clingers, burrowers, swimmers, and crawlers. They live under rocks and in other sheltered places out of the current and out of reach of trout and other predators.

When the time and temperature are right, hatching occurs. Some species crawl out of the water onto stones or twigs to hatch, but most species struggle or swim to the surface where, as soon as their thorax breaks through the surface film, their skin splits and in the twinkling of an eye the water-breathing creature magically becomes an air-breathing creature!

Now a dun, or subimago, the mayfly rests where it is until its wings are dry, an elapsed time that can be measured in seconds. If the weather includes cold temperatures, rain, or wind, however, it may keep the dun on the water longer—for minutes perhaps—during which time it will be easy prey for the trout. Once its wings are dry, the dun flies to vegetation. There, in twenty-four to forty-eight hours, it will again shed its skin and become the mature spinner, the imago. The dun, with opaque wings, can be thought of as the "teenager" and the spinner, with clear wings, as the sexually mature adult.

Male and female spinners congregate in separate areas and the female, when ready to mate, finds the waiting males "dancing up and down" in anticipation and mates with one of them, the copulation taking place in the air. Some mayflies mate over land and others over the water. Upon completion of mating the female will deposit some or all of her eggs by various methods, again according to species. These include dipping down to drop them on the water's surface, resting on the surface, or even crawling into the water on rocks or branches to deposit the eggs on the stream bottom. When she has deposited all the eggs the female will either die on the stream or return to the land to die, depending on the species. On the water, she will be known as a "spent spinner," or "spent wing," her wings spread flat on the surface.

The duns fly directly from the stream to vegetation, so it is usually the spinners you will see in the air over the water. Mayflies can be identified by their wings, two large and two small, and an up-and-down flight pattern.

The angler, then, may need to match her fly to any one of the appropriate stages: the nymph, the dun as an emerger and then again after it is out of the shuck waiting for its wings to dry, the female spinner with and without the egg sac, and the spent wing.

Caddisflies

Caddisflies boast the Latin name *Trichoptera*, which means "hair wings"; they are also called sedges. At rest with their four wings folded over their backs they look like little pup tents. The eggs hatch

Caddis larvae can be identified by their cases made of sticks and pebbles. After leaving the cases they come to the surface in air bubbles as fully formed adults.

into wormlike larvae. This stage is best known for the cases the larvae construct for themselves out of tiny sticks and stones held together by their own threadlike secretions. These cases are easy to identify and caddis are amazingly abundant. You'll find them crawling about on the underside of streambed rocks.

Inside the case, the larvae change to pupae a week or two before emergence. Then, at the "birthing" time, they change to adults and come out of their homes encased in a bubble of air for a free ride to the surface (it sounds like a space program) where, when their wings dry, they fly away. With four wings of the same length, caddis have a mothlike appearance and their flight pattern is relatively level as they move in swarms in an upstream direction.

Caddis mating takes place in streamside vegetation and, when ready, the female returns to the stream to deposit her eggs.

The stages to match with your fly are cased, emerging pupa, and adult, both fluttering and at rest. One of my expert-at-nymphing friends, Bob Good of Denver, originated the Colorado Caddis pattern.

It is an uncased larva worm and can be very effective, even though the incidence of uncased caddis must be exceedingly small.

Stoneflies

Stoneflies, called *Plecoptera* in Latin, which means "folded wing," look just plain "buggy" at maturity. They are easily identifiable at rest with their three body segments, three pairs of jointed legs with claws, antennae, two tails, and four wings folded over their backs. They look like the kind of insects that might have been found in cave-dweller's art.

From the eggs the stoneflies hatch into nymphs and go through several molts as they mature. When ready for emergence, they crawl out of the water to rest on stones, sticks, and logs. They then shuck their skins (look for their cases) and move into the vegetation.

Probably because they are weak fliers, mating does not take place in flight. At egg-depositing time, when the stoneflies must fly, trout

Stonefly life cycle, clockwise from bottom right: nymph, nymphal case, newly hatched adult, and adults.

Midges are much smaller than other aquatic insects, but what they lack in size they make up for in numbers. The underwater larvae and pupae and the reproducing adults are all taken readily by trout. This drawing depicts a meadow stream environment.

are given their best shot at the adults. Otherwise, it is the nymphal form that is most available. Because there are one-, two-, and even three- to four-year varieties, there are always some fair-size immature stoneflies in the stream in which they occur. There are, then, just two stages to imitate: the nymph and the adult.

The cool, fast-running, well-oxygenated streams of Montana, like the Bighorn and Madison, produce the most famous stonefly hatch in America, known strangely as the *salmon fly* hatch. Enormous two- to three-inch-long nymphs, and adults with a three-inch wingspan, create great excitement among fish and fishermen, and many anglers make annual June pilgrimages to the Rockies for this very special experience.

Midges

Midges have the Latin name of *Diptera*, which means "apart" plus "wing." These are true flies—tiny, mosquitolike insects with two transparent wings. They rarely get larger than three-eighths of an inch as larvae and are less than one-half inch long even in the biggest adults. What they lack in size, however, they make up for in numbers. Just like bears eating blueberries, the trout take them by the mouthful. There are thousands of species of diptera, including the black flies that love to feast on fishermen, but midges are the important one to anglers. These are tied on #16 to #24 hooks.

Underwater, as larvae, midges are poor swimmers and drift with the current when they are dislodged from the bottom sediment or rock crevices. This is when they are first accessible to trout. When larvae swim to the surface as pupae, they do so with a slow wiggle and make an easy meal. As they drift on the surface after escaping their shuck, they are again an easy mark. Finally they fly, but their mating and egg laying occurs over water. Bonanza! Trout have access to them in all stages of their lives, and in large numbers. On tiny hooks, your imitations don't have to be very accurate for the larvae, pupae, and adults, but using the right size is important. Don't worry about actual color, just whether the fly is light or dark.

Terrestrials

Lots of wonderful food drops off banks, is washed in by floods, falls out of trees, and is blown in by wind. Worms, grubs, beetles, ants, grasshoppers, and anything else that lives near a stream can be food for trout. While most of these terrestrials are available throughout the season, they become more important in the summer, after the major mayfly hatches have ended.

Pattern Selection

The flies you'll carry are divided into just two categories: naturals and attractors. Naturals are the ones that match the hatch, so to speak, or look like a bug that might exist. Attractors are flies that don't exist in nature but catch fish. They work when there is no insect activity (and sometimes when there is), and they work almost anywhere the lure of trout fishing takes you: east, west, Europe, Argentina, New Zealand! Attractors are your backup patterns.

Attractors work because, familiar or not, they look alive. Movement expresses life to all of nature's creatures and, knowing he can eject it, the trout takes it into his mouth perhaps just to satisfy his curiosity.

There are two types of motion that make the artificial fly attractive to a trout: motion within the fly and motion that you or the stream imparts to the fly. Motion within the fly itself is determined by its

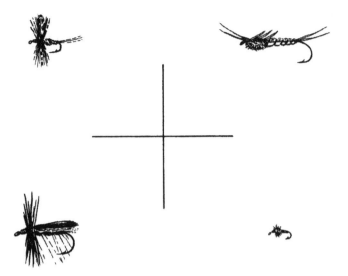

Naturals. Clockwise from top left: Adams #16, Brown Stone Fly Nymph #10, Midge Pupa #20, Henryville Caddis #10.

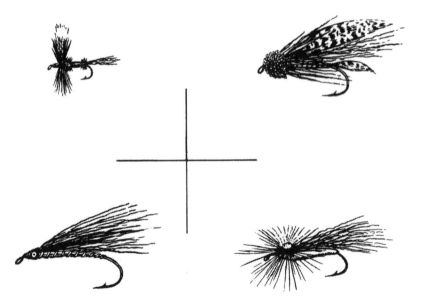

Attractors. Clockwise from top left: Royal Wulff #14, Muddler Minnow #6, Surface Stone Fly #8, Mickey Finn #4.

construction, by the materials used to simulate the movement of gills in nymphs or of legs in adults. Motion that you or the stream's flow gives to the fly is done with line manipulation or use of the current. An artificial nymph seems alive with a twitch of the line or a lifting of the rod tip. A streamer cast quartering downstream swims across the current.

When it comes to choosing which flies to carry, you can fill several vests with imitations to cover all the stages of all the individual species that might be available to trout, or you can carry some naturals and some attractors as a basic selection, then buy whatever else might work when and as you need them. In this way just one vest will do, although all anglers buy and carry more flies than they'll ever use.

It's the uncertainty that keeps us filling up the boxes . . . *which* fly do I dare not carry? And then there are those special flies that you had to have once. For me, one pattern is the aforementioned Colorado Caddis, which knocked 'em dead on Colorado's Elk River in 1975 and has never worked for me in the East since. Lee carries a little green inchworm imitation that was once the prime "hatch" on a Pennsylvania river during his early years. You'll have your own special-occasion flies and the stories to explain their presence. It's part of the fun of fly fishing.

Art Flick's *Streamside Guide to Naturals and Their Imitations* is the simple bible to eastern mayfly hatches. Flick, during a three-year study in New York's Catskill Mountains, chronicled the sequence of important hatches, which are only about a dozen. They are Quill Gordon, Hendrickson/Red Quill (female/male), Cream Variant (known as Dorothea), Red Quill, American March Brown, Grey Fox, Light Cahill, Green Drake, Dun variant (Isonychia), Light Grey Fox variant, and Blue-Winged Olive.

The duplication of the Red Quill means that using the same artificial will work for both hatches. This brings up something of a puzzle that many anglers have observed. There are many reference books that show photographs of the real insects and of the flies used to imitate them. Very often there is no real likeness between male and female versions or between imitation and natural. This makes me think that although these particular imitations caught fish when those naturals were on the water, might not some other imitation have worked just as well? Perhaps it's not quite as scientific as we may have been led to believe.

The following chart will give you an idea of the flies to carry. The chart is divided into what is appropriate in the eastern and western sections of the United States and the hook sizes that are most likely to work.

A Basic Selection of Dry Flies

Fly Type	East	West
Mayflies	#16, #14 Adams	#16, #14 Adams
	#14, #12 Royal Wulff	#12, #10 Royal Wulff
	#16 Quill Gordon	#12 Goofus Bug
	#14 Hendrickson	#16, #18 Pale Evening Dun
	#14 Light Cahill	#16, #18 Pale Morning Dun
	#12 March Brown	#14 Parachute
	#16, #14 Variants: grey, cream, and brown	#16 Blue-Winged Olive
Caddisflies	#16 Henryville Caddis	#14 Elk Hair Caddis
	#14 Chuck Caddis	
	#14, #12 Bivisible	
Stoneflies	#12 Yellow Stonefly	#8 Sofa Pillow
	#10 Surface Stone Fly	#8 Surface Stone Fly
Midges	#20 Griffith's Gnat	#20 Griffith's Gnat

The Adams and Royal Wulff are two flies I wouldn't be without wherever I fish for trout. The Adams looks buggy and is unbelievably effective almost any time. The Royal Wulff is an attractor I use as a "search" fly when no fish are rising. I also use it in the evening because I can see its white wings!

Here is a list of wet flies to include:

Fly Type	East	West
Wet Flies	#14, #12 Hare's Ear	#12 Hare's Ear
	#14, #12 Royal Coachman	#12, #10 Royal Coachman
	#12 Black Gnat	#12 Black Gnat

You'll notice that many of the flies are listed as both East and West. The trout and insect life in western rivers tend to be larger than those in the East. Consequently, the size of the fly is generally larger and can be more heavily dressed.

You will also need nymphs and streamers. Here are my suggestions:

Fly Type	East	West
Nymphs	#14 Small Grey Nymph	#12 Zug Bug
	#20 Pheasant Tail	#20 Pheasant Tail
	#12 Zug Bug	#8 Brown Stone
	#10 Brown Stone	#6 Montana Stone
	#10 Strawman	#14 Hare's Ear
	#12 Flymph	#12 Flymph
	#14, #12 Sparkle Pupa	#14, #12 Sparkle Pupa
	#20, #24 Midge pupa and larva	#20, #24 Midge pupa and larva
Streamers *et al.*	#6 Black Ghost	#4 Grey Ghost
	#8 Black-Nosed Dace	#8, #6 Leeches
	#4 Mickey Finn	#8, #6 Woolly Buggers
	#6, #8 Muddlers	#6 Muddlers

Streamers are minnow or baitfish imitations. Muddlers, Leeches, and Woolly Buggers represent other aquatic life or something that could be real.

Terrestrials to include are:

Fly Type	East	West
Terrestrials	#16 Ants	#14 Ants
	#10, #8 Woolly Worm	#8 Woolly Worm
	#14, #12 Humpy	#12, #10 Humpy
	#10, #6 Grasshoppers	#8, #6 Grasshoppers
	#16 Beetles	

Don't load up on hatch imitations until you've acquired some knowledge about the insect life of the streams you'll fish. Many anglers never get to fish hatches. Until I moved to New York's Beaverkill area, hatches were something I read and dreamed of and thought everyone else experienced regularly. Not so. If your area is not big on mayfly hatches, your basic selection might be more like the following list. If I had to choose ten flies I could "live or die with" I'd choose these:

Adams #14 or #18
Royal Wulff #12
Black-Nosed Dace #4
Chuck Caddis #10
Zug Bug #10
Brown Stonefly nymph #8
Muddler Minnow #6
Ant #16
Blue-Winged Olive #20
Surface Stone Fly #10

With this limited number of patterns you need scissors and a dark-colored magic marker to adapt them as needed. You can change the character of a fly by trimming off the wings, the above-water hackles, or everything but the body (to make a pupa). It's hard to make a dark fly light, but with your marker you could certainly make a light fly dark.

The Surface Stone Fly is a special fly. It is made with a body of plastic molded on a hook. The hair and feathers are embedded in the body, not tied. It is a method invented by Lee and the pattern was developed for Atlantic salmon. I first used it successfully for trout in a #10 during a green drake hatch on the Beaverkill. The Surface Stone Fly floats in the surface film and, on that occasion, looked like the shuck of the green drake. It can also be fished underwater like a streamer and, as with the Muddler Minnow, the Surface Stone Fly's silhouette is different from all other flies.

When friends speak of aquatic insects by their Latin names, it can be totally intimidating. There are common names for most of them, so just ask, "Which fly is that in the *Streamside Guide* or in the local tackle shop?" If you can identify the insect group, you can usually make do by then matching size and color. The only difficulty with this system may be in asking for replacements when you've lost your supply or when you're speaking about the fishing action with other anglers.

I think you'll find, as I have, that through experience and observation of particular insect activity you will gradually come to know the names of the important ones. In many ways it's like going to a party of strangers; you'll know all about a select handful when you leave—Miss Baetis, Mr. Isonychia, and the Hexagenias—but others will look familiar when next you meet.

If the trout are taking insects in something other than the mature

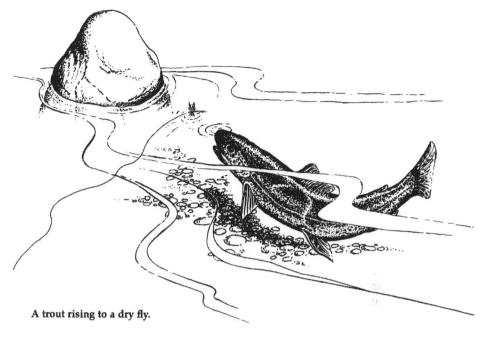

A trout rising to a dry fly.

form, you must look for clues as to which fly to use based on your knowledge of the stages in which the trout have access. If, for example, the trout are flashing but not breaking the surface, they are probably feeding on nymphs on the bottom or in the next stage, as they start to rise to the surface.

There are various kinds and intensities of surface and subsurface rises, from bulges to leaps. As a general rule, quiet takes mean that the trout know the insects are less likely to escape, and these might be midge pupae in the surface film or spent spinners. Noisy takes mean the opposite: Hurry while you can catch them; the trout are after emerging caddis or egg-laying adults of all groups.

This general coverage should give you an idea of why so much has been written about trout fishing. Specifics on all this information are readily available, both locally and in books, magazines, and videos. Getting better at catching trout is a series of discoveries that everyone goes through. When writers discover something, they write about it. I think, though, that some experience is necessary before what you read can really help you. You can't remember everything and much of what you read may be superfluous. Experience helps you be discerning and is the glue that puts it all together.

Make it your own experience. If all your fishing is in the company of others but you have an idea of the many ways in which a trout can be caught, cut the cord and *go fishing alone!* And go as often as you can.

Independence is the goal in all aspects of our lives. We can get more and give more by being independent and by making decisions and being comfortable with them. From early on in my fishing career I have almost exclusively fished with men who were exceptional fishermen. In the early years I felt intimidated and so, for a time, fell into the trap of depending on them. It happens to others.

Recently, a friend who is dating a more experienced fisherman told me about a session they had on the Beaverkill. He caught the first fish. She asked what he was using. He told her. She put that fly on. They continued fishing. She saw him catch more fish while she was shut out. Half an hour later she complained that the fly hadn't worked for her. His reply: "Oh, they stopped taking that fly and I changed to such and such." This kind of experience (which I have had) makes you feel frustrated. Being dependent can freeze you in the learning process. If you never take the responsibility, you never get the reward. Don't fall into this trap!

Fishing alone changes this. You have no one to answer to except yourself, and your competition is with the fish. You will be more aware; you'll think more "like a fish" when left to your own devices. You'll be building your own knowledge, one step at a time, knowing what *you* did that worked, not what someone else did. There is more than one way to catch a trout and you'll find it. Fishing alone will do a lot for you.

Competition is hard to avoid when fishing with other anglers. If you find it a burden, however, you can decide not to do it until you have gained confidence and feel that you are ready. Then it can be fun as well as beneficial in sharpening your senses and skills.

I don't mean to put down companionship. There is nothing nicer than fishing with a friend with whom your relationship is comfortable. Sharing the experience heightens your enjoyment. It also puts it in its proper perspective; fly fishing is a sport that constantly humbles you. You must be able to laugh at yourself and the predicaments we all get into with our tackle, from catching our fly in a tree on the first backcast to losing a good fish on a "wind knot," or having a trout run between our legs at the landing.

And, if you are serious about a relationship with a someone, it's the best testing ground I know. Your real values, of fairness, honesty, self-reliance, consideration of others, and genuine regard for the outdoors are exposed for all to see when you spend time in the trout's world.

10

The Anadromous Fish: Atlantic Salmon, Pacific Salmon, and Steelhead

Because the salmon is the most stately fish that a man can angle for in fresh water, therefore I intend to begin with him. The salmon is a noble fish, but he is cumbersome to catch. For generally he is only in deep places of great rivers, and for the most part he keeps to the middle of the water, so that a man cannot come at him. And he is in season from March until Michaelmas . . . you may catch him (but this is seldom seen) with an artificial fly at such times as he leaps as you catch a trout or a grayling.

Atlantic Salmon

Salmo salar, the leaper! Noble in Dame Juliana's time, magnificent in ours. Salar is the greatest game fish that swims in the minds of all who angle for him.

Every kind of fishing has its special challenges and joys, but wading a stream with light tackle for big fish has to be one of the most rewarding. The anadromous species, which include Atlantic and

Pacific salmon, steelhead, shad, and sea-run trout, give us this opportunity. They are born in fresh water, grow to adulthood in salt water, and return to fresh water to spawn. The species are different from each other in their life cycles and in their tendency to take a fly, but because they are ocean travelers all have an air of mystique about them.

Atlantic salmon are found in Canada's Atlantic provinces and the state of Maine and are being restored to some other states in New England. Iceland is famous for its salmon fishing, as are Norway, Scotland, and Ireland. Russia's Kola Peninsula is expected to be the Atlantic salmon hot spot during the 1990s.

These salmon spend two to four years or more in the stream of their birth as parr before turning silver and going to sea as 6-inch smolt. If they return after one year of sea-feeding, they will weigh from 2½ to 5 pounds and will be "grilse." If they stay at sea for two years, or possibly three, they will return as salmon, weighing from about 10 pounds upward. Salmon have been caught that weighed more than 50 pounds.

After their long sea journey, Atlantics will return not only to the river of their birth but even to the particular pool they inhabited. Depending on their country of origin, they enter fresh water anytime from February to the end of September for a late fall spawning, during which time they will not eat. Nature shuts off their digestive system, and it is thought that not more than 20 percent of all salmon who reach the spawning beds survive. It is an arduous journey. If they do survive, they will return to the sea (and are sometimes caught on the way back downstream as "black salmon") to grow even larger before the next spawning.

Atlantic salmon return to the streams of their birth supercharged with energy and at the peak of their physical fitness. Restless to complete their mission, but forced to wait for the actual spawning time, they are aware of anything and everything in their environment. With all that pent-up energy they porpoise and roll and leap and occasionally take our artificial flies into their mouths, probably intending to spit them out again.

The reason why salmon take artificial flies has been a source of discussion among salmon anglers since Dame Juliana's time. Increasingly it is thought to be an action triggered by memories, or reflexes, developed in their years as parr when they ate everything they could get into their mouths. Whatever the reason, it gives us our sport.

Salmon rivers are usually big rivers, and you may be fishing from a canoe rather than wading. Either way you can use the same patterns of presentation on Atlantic salmon that you use on trout. Most salmon

Hitching a Salmon Fly

Half hitch #1   Half hitch #2

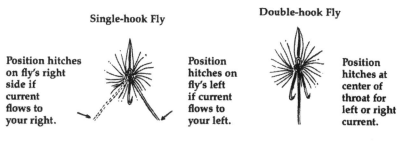

Single-hook Fly   **Double-hook Fly**

Position hitches on fly's right side if current flows to your right.

Position hitches on fly's left if current flows to your left.

Position hitches at center of throat for left or right current.

fishermen use the time-honored technique of quartering downstream to swim wet flies across the current. You can make the fishing more interesting by "hitching" a wet fly to make it skim on the surface. After the fly is attached to your leader, throw two interlocking half-hitches over the head of the fly and position them at an angle determined by the direction of the river's flow. The wake created by the hitched fly is attractive to both the fisherman and the fish. It gives the angler something to watch, and the salmon must break the surface to take it, which is always exciting.

If you know where a salmon is lying because you have seen him roll or porpoise, dry flies can give thrilling action. Sometimes the fish will come up right next to the fly, or swat it with his tail or move it with his nose, and not take it! It makes your feet come right up off the stream's bottom when that head breaks the surface next to your dry fly. This playful behavior has led to the following definition: You have reached full maturity as a salmon fisherman when you can watch a salmon break the surface right next to your fly with his mouth open, not take the fly and submerge again, without striking! That's a tough maturity to reach.

Another special technique is to use a dry-fly skater as a search fly. Fish it quartering downstream with a floating line and greased leader;

when it comes under tension, it will skim across the surface. You can give the skater an erratic action, if you wish, by lifting and lowering or vibrating your rod as it moves across the current. This skating technique really excites salmon and produces the most spectacular rises I've ever seen.

One of the most interesting experiences I have had to date with salmon and various flies occurred on the Grand Cascapedia River in Quebec. We were fishing Big Curly, a long, slow, bathtublike pool among majestic rocks, and there were several dozen large salmon swimming lazily within it. It was an unusual fishing condition for me. I started with a large black ant designed by Lee to help him prove that Atlantic salmon would take terrestrials. After the whole school had looked at it, they backed off, altering their pattern a bit. I changed the character of the fly, going to a Wulff, then a bomber, and then to traditionals. Unbelievably, each first or second cast would bring all of the salmon in the pool to look at the fly and then they'd back off again. After six or seven fly changes I was very frustrated and had an eerie feeling about the level of their sensitivity. No dumb fish, these! They saw us as well as we saw them and were curious about the "insects" that were invading their territory.

I finally went back to the big black ant just before we were to leave the pool. I cast it well away from the visible salmon, looked toward them for a second and then back at the fly to see a hole in the water where it had been. The fish that took it was a nice 14-pound male and that gave me even more to think about.

I much prefer not to see the fish I'm seeking. I like the surprise of the head breaking the surface or the sudden underwater take telegraphed to my hand. Visible salmon are usually difficult to bring to the fly. They sometimes require dozens of casts and then, if you've made 167 presentations and quit, you always wonder if it would have taken number 168.

Once you've hooked an Atlantic salmon, another facet of the fun begins! They are fish of the open water and don't try to hide under logs or other debris—they make spectacular jumps and reel-screaming runs up and down the river, while you try to keep up with them. Having used their swiftness to outdistance seals and other ocean predators, they can sometimes be more than you can handle, but it is fantastically exhilarating to find yourself attached to one of these majestic fish!

When choosing your tackle start with a 7-weight outfit: a 9-foot rod weighing 3 ounces or less, a #7 weight-forward or #6/7 triangle-taper floating line, a 9-foot leader ending at 10-pound-test, and a selection of flies.

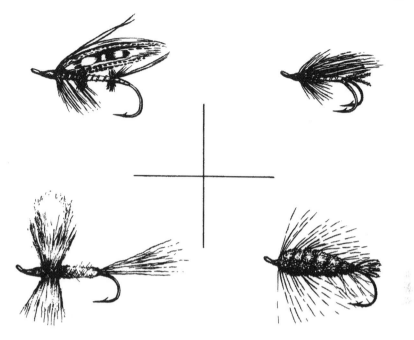

Salmon flies. Clockwise from top left: Jock Scott #4, Rusty Rat #8, Bomber #4, White Wulff #6.

Traditionals should include the following:

Blue Charm
Green Highlander
Jock Scott
Silver Blue
Thunder and Lightning
Mar Lodge
Hairy Mary

Other flies to include are:

Rusty Rat
Silver Rat
Cosseboom
Royal, White, and Grey Wulffs
Lady Joan
Wulff Surface Stone Fly
Bombers

Fly sizes range from #8 to 4/0. Larger flies are used in the early season when the water is high. These require heavy lines to be cast easily. You can get by up to a certain point with careful casting on your light tackle, but you might want to back yourself up with an 8/9-weight outfit for this situation.

Atlantic salmon fishing can be demanding because it might include deep wading, hundreds of casts a day, rocky shores waiting to emasculate your flies, and black flies. (Only Iceland seems not to have biting insects on its rivers.) But we keep coming back for more.

The word that characterizes this fishing best is *uncertainty*. An absolute novice can outfish experienced anglers the first time out. It's a bit like a hole-in-one early in your golf game; it's not as easy as it seemed the next time on the course. Over the long run, good fishermen outfish poor ones, but even the best salmon fisherman in the world can be blanked for unexplained reasons.

Salmon guides and anglers spend most of the time they are together, before, during, and after the fishing, talking about why the fish took their flies or why they didn't. There's a lot more to talk about during bad conditions and one of a guide's job requirements must be to come up with a great variety of reasons, given solemnly and with great compassion, as to why the salmon are not taking the angler's flies. Here are some you will encounter:

water is too low
water is too high
water is too cold
water is too warm
water level is falling
water level is rising
peat-colored water
muddy water from rain
wind from wrong direction
barometer is falling
too sunny
thunderstorm coming
in the river too long
moved upriver last night
fished too hard
haven't got the right fly
air is colder than the water
jumping salmon never take
traveling fish won't take
not where they're supposed to be

"They *should* be taking!"
"Can't understand it!"
"There are no fish!"

When there are fish and they might be taking flies, here are some "helpful" maxims that add to the mystique of Atlantic salmon fishing:

1. On dull days use dull flies.

2. On bright days use bright flies.

3. As spawning time nears, males will respond to larger, gaudier flies.

4. Male fish fight harder than do females.

5. After a "touch," or "prick," wait two or three minutes before trying the same fish again.

6. Never leave a fish you have risen without offering the fly he rose to one last time.

7. Say "God Save the Queen" before striking.

8. Instead of striking with a tight line, let slip six inches of line on the take.

9. A salmon that takes a dry fly doesn't close his mouth until he's gone back to his lie.

As you may well imagine, many of these are controversial, and number 9 is said to also apply to steelhead. I'll tell you my experience along that line in the section on steelhead.

Pacific Salmon

There are two major differences between Atlantic and Pacific salmon, and they are of utmost importance to the fly angler. The first is that the Atlantics may survive their spawning. The Pacifics begin to change chemically when they enter fresh water, deteriorating at a speed relative to actual spawning time, after which they must die. The second is that the tendency to take a fly is inherent in Atlantics; Pacifics go to sea at a much younger age and so are not patterned to take insects on or near the surface when they return to fresh water. Of the five Pacific species—chinook, coho, sockeye, pink, and chum—the coho is most likely to take a fly. The 7- to 15-pound fish are great fun on a fly rod when they first enter the streams and will succumb to big streamers.

I have no experience with the other species but am sure that when they first come into fresh water there is some chance of catching them with flies, even if you have to use weight in the fly or on the leader. Everyone should fish for Pacifics at least once. There is no other fishing like it because it answers the hunger in all of us for that angler's heaven on earth where you are surrounded by great masses of large fish. It is only challenge that is missing with the Pacifics; there is very little uncertainty here. In its place, because of the numbers and size of the salmon, is just plain *awe*.

A 7-weight outfit might work for cohos if the fish are close in and the wind isn't blowing, but again, an 8/9 may be better. The species that grows the largest, the king salmon, are best handled with 9- or 10-weight tackle. Effective flies are streamer types with Flashabou or other material that simulates the iridescence of baitfish.

Steelhead

Steelhead are my new and second love in anadromous fish. They are beautiful, as in rainbow-trout beautiful, but can weigh up to 30 pounds. Although steelhead are now found in the tributaries of the Great Lakes, they are native to my favorite area of the continent for scenery: our own Pacific northwest and British Columbia. The wadable, glacier-fed rivers of "B.C." are particularly fitting for these great fish that can be taken with surface flies.

The usual method is to make the cast quartering downstream and then to immediately mend the line against the current to slow the fly's speed. Steelhead like their flies moving at a slower speed than do trout or Atlantic salmon, so whenever the rod tip gets very far ahead of the fly, you mend back against the current and try to keep the rod tip, the fly line, and the fly in a straight line, parallel to the banks as they move across the current. Wet flies can be fished this way, and a deer-hair floater will "wake" across the surface (like the hitched wet flies for Atlantic salmon) at a speed attractive to the steelhead.

When you hear of "dry-fly-caught" steelhead, this "waking" is usually what is meant. (I find this term misleading in that dry-fly-caught, to me, means dead-drifted dry flies.) Happily, it is possible to take steelhead by dead-drifting a dry fly; with only two opportunities to try it, I have hooked two and landed one and loved every minute.

The story of that second fish may be helpful. I always strike a dry-fly-taking fish with a speed prompted by the speed of his strike and what I see of his physical proportions. Lee and I were fishing the upper Copper River out of Martin Schmidderer's fishing lodge near Terrace, B.C., and I had spoken to guide Bob Hull of having once hooked and later lost a steelhead on a dead-drifted dry fly. On this particular afternoon, Bob and I had worked upriver of Lee and, in scanning a new piece of water, we saw a steelhead rise. We looked at each other with delight and I put a #8 Orange Bomber on my leader.

The fish boiled at the fly on the first drift. Another boil on the second drift. I changed to a #10 Royal Wulff. He took it and I set the hook. Nothing to it? Nothing there! As I stood staring at my returned fly, Bob was yelling at me, "Don't strike until he's gone back to his lie!" "Are you kidding?" I asked. "No, he holds the fly but doesn't close his mouth tightly until he gets where he's going. You pulled it out!" (Shades of one of the Atlantic salmon maxims.) I remembered how I had hooked my first dryfly steelhead, which went just fine without any delay in striking, and didn't really believe what Bob was saying. To make a long story shorter, I drifted the fly again. No take. Bob told me to change flies. I put on a White Wulff. A take. I waited a second or two and came up with another empty hook. "Too soon!" he yelled.

Two steelhead takes to a dry fly! Would I ever be given another chance? I had nothing to lose at that point. "If the god of fishes ever sees fit to bring another fish to my fly while I'm with you," I promised, "I won't strike until you tell me to." Bob wanted more. "Here, put on this Sofa Pillow fly." I did. Believe it or not, the fish, or another that was with him, took the fly. Three takes! Somebody up there liked me. There seemed to be a big hole in the water as I waited, frozen in time, for Bob to say the word. All signs of the fish had vanished when he said "now" three full seconds later. I tightened gently and damned if he wasn't on! It was a 13- to 14-pound male and he headed downstream to give me some interesting problems in the fast water for the next fifteen minutes.

I took that fish and others on a waking fly while using a Graphite III 8½-foot rod that weighed less than 3 ounces and was rated for a #5 line. Because of the stiffness of the rod, I experimented and found that a triangle taper 6/7 did not overload it but, instead, brought it to life. So, once again, the recommendation is to start with a 6- or 7-weight outfit, not going heavier until there is some reason to do so. A 9-foot rod will be better for the necessary mending than anything shorter. A 9-foot leader tapered to 1X will do as your base leader.

Steelhead flies are often named for the rivers on which they were originated. Names such as Babine Special, Skykomish Sunrise, Silver Rogue, Mad River, Rogue River Special all indicate this. Among the dozens of others are names such as Polar Shrimp, Pink Lady,

Parmachene Belle, Horrible Matuka, and even a McGinty. It's always good to buy the important local flies, but the same Bombers, Muddler Minnows, and Wulff dry flies you use for Atlantic salmon should be in your vest.

The life cycle and spawning habits of steelhead are not as well chronicled as are those of Atlantic salmon. The late Roderick Haig-Brown, an Englishman who spent most of his adult life on British Columbia's Vancouver Island, is the best-known writer of books on the subject of steelhead and their rivers.

I recently met a Californian who fishes for steelhead in the Gualala River in the northern part of the state. To get there before dawn, so that she can claim an all-day spot in the river, she leaves home at 1:30 A.M. Arriving in Santa Rosa, she breakfasts and then puts on her waders in her car under the lights of the restaurant's parking lot.

At 5:30 A.M. she arrives at the river and, with the company of a flashlight, walks through the dark, rather spooky woods avoiding broken beer bottles and other trash. The area is noted for vandalism and many fishermen's cars are broken into. Although she knows some of the regular fishermen, she stays until dark, whether she is the last one in the river or not, then runs to her car and drives off in her waders to change again in some parking lot in town.

I asked her why she didn't at least come off the river with another angler if she didn't feel quite safe. "I'd lose some of the fishing," she said. "Having the river to myself is the important thing."

Other Species

My experience with other anadromous fish, such as sea-run browns and shad, is quite limited. The browns are next on my list of new challenges. They hit a fly like lightning and must be wonderful to catch in sizes larger than the 2-pounders I've caught incidentally while fishing for Atlantic salmon. The best tales of sea-run browns come out of southern Argentina.

Shad come into most of the East Coast's rivers, from Florida north. The earliest ones are taken on weighted flies. They are better appreciated for their delectable roe than for their fighting abilities when hooked, but a large river like the nearby Delaware can create challenges for the angler with any species. Shad will take surface flies as the water warms.

All anadromous fish are most challenging when they are fresh from the sea, still bright silver in color and perhaps with a few sea lice on them. That's when all of the romance of their travels comes into focus.

11

From the Strike to the Capture

When Lee and I moved from New Hampshire to the banks of New York's Beaverkill River in the Catskills, we brought with us our four-year-old male cat. We hoped with all our hearts that he could adjust to living in a new area that was just as wild as his original home. During the breaking-in period I had the idea to put a leash on him and attach it to a tree so he wouldn't disappear.

I carefully fastened the collar on Gus, although he was fighting it all the way, and then held the other end of the leash. What happened next was explosive! He ran the full extent of its length, did a somersault, then ran in the opposite direction and did another somersault, rolled on the ground trying to rub the collar off his neck, jumped into the air twice more and succeeded in escaping that which had tethered him for the first time in his very full life.

He was just like a game fish! I found myself "playing" him, my senses fully alert, my arm and body leaning with his pressures. When he jumped, I gave him as much slack in the leash as possible so that I wouldn't choke him. When it was over, I understood for the first time, in a very graphic way, why a fish behaves as he does when hooked.

It is the tethering of a wild creature, not hook pain, that sends a trout or a tarpon into a series of spectacular jumps or triggers the hundred-yard dash of a bonefish across the shallow flats. Fish are cold-blooded creatures, so their nervous system is not as highly developed as that of humans. If you or I had a hook in our mouth, the last thing we would do would be to run in the opposite direction, increasing the pressure. I'd go right to the source of my pain and hope it would be eliminated. When a fish is tethered by a hook, it will do just as Gus did—use all of its wiles and energy to escape.

A knowledgeable angler can often counteract these efforts by a change in position, rod angle, or pressure, and play a fish quickly enough so no harm will be done. Fish are not harmed by being caught. They are harmed by being played to complete exhaustion or, when taken from the water, by being squeezed too hard, being held by the gills, or careless removal of the hook.

Striking

The strike is a special moment in time, and it makes my spirits soar. For some people, landing the fish is the high point of the whole experience, but for me the strike is the moment that is the most precious. It means everything was right!

A fraction of an inch is all the movement it takes to sink the hook point, or barb, into a fish's mouth. To do this, an instant of tension must be created by eliminating any slack line between the angler and the fish. This sometimes requires the combined action of the rod hand and the line hand.

The technique of fishing downstream keeps the fly and line under tension as it moves across the current. When a fish takes the fly and turns to go back to his feeding place, he essentially hooks himself. To make sure, though, it is wise to respond "in kind" with a strike about as hard as his take felt—if he gives you the chance before surging away.

Upstream techniques for dry flies or unweighted nymphs require the attention of the angler at the strike. Slack has been employed to let the flies float freely, so the elimination of that slack on the sensed or visually triggered strike must be a reflex action. Both your hands respond. As the rod tip is lifted up or moved to one side, the line hand pulls in the opposite direction to remove the slack until an absolute connection is felt. Then another reflex action is required: You need to relax the tension immediately.

It is a good idea to practice slack line strikes. Choose a large dry fly that's easy to see, such as a #12 white Wulff. Make the presentation. Keep your eyes on the fly, then imagine strikes at different places in the drift, each of which might entail different amounts of slack leader or line. Analyze the amount of effort required to bring the hook under tension. It must move only a fraction of an inch in the fish's mouth. To simulate hook penetration of the cartilage, practice with two or three inches of movement. You'll realize the importance of holding the fly line under a finger of your rod hand and of picking up slack with your line hand as the fly drifts. As you practice you'll make small adjustments in your overall readiness. Your mental condition should be one of relaxed alertness.

With practice you will also learn if the rod should be moved up or to the side on the strike. You'll see that the line length, the amount of slack, and whether the fly is upstream, across stream, or slightly downstream of you will affect your decision. Practice striking with these various factors until nothing can catch you by surprise.

Nine times out of ten the fish will be hooked on the side of its mouth that was nearest to you when he took the fly. Picture him facing upstream. As he takes the fly, its connection to you, plus the strike, will move it toward you so it hooks in that side of his jaw. Whenever you land a fish, check to see if this is true. This knowledge can be important in the playing and landing of a big fish: You cannot put maximum pressure on him from any side but the one on which he is hooked without the danger of pulling or working the hook out of his mouth.

Playing Fish

> *If you have the fortune to hook a great fish with a small tackle, you must lead him in the water and labor with him there until he is overcome and wearied. Then take him as well as you can, and beware that you do not hold beyond the strength of your line. . . . do not let him come out of the end of your line straight from you, but keep him always under the rod, and always hold him strait, so that your line can sustain and bear his leaps and his plunges with the help of your hand.*

Poor Juliana didn't have a reel from which a fish could run off extra line. The strength of the line was very important because it was all there was. We use monofilament leaders that stretch a bit, but you must not "hold beyond the strength" of its weakest part, which is the tippet next to the fly.

Oh how I wish Juliana and I could fish together. She could use my state-of-the-art graphite 6-weight, and I could borrow her hazel, willow, or aspen rod with horsehair line. We might talk about which outfit was most sensitive to the fish's every move, which kept us in closer touch, and which let us feel its every heartbeat better than the other.

Women have natural attributes for playing fish. We have patience and sensitivity. We have enough strength for the task, but not so much that we feel we can dominate through it. Women are much less likely to lose fish during the playing than are men unless they are hesitant or don't know when to exert heavy pressure and, therefore, are never in command of the situation.

If you have no plan or show no skill, you are likely to fall victim to a companion or guide who is forever yelling at you to do this or that. No matter what the psychological pressure, *don't do anything that doesn't feel right!* Take advice but don't take orders. Unless you really understand the instructions, don't give up the responsibility unless you are just over your head. It's a no-man's land unless you have given some thought to the playing process *before* you've hooked the largest fish of your life. Along with your tactical knowledge, trust your instincts. It's not life and death you are dealing with; it's the fun of playing a fish, whatever the outcome.

Angler Nancy Phipps of Tallahassee, Florida, has complete confidence in her ability to play Atlantic salmon, and when her Scottish ghillie yells instructions, she finds that she simply cannot hear him for the rush of the river's noise.

Slack

Now, though, the fish is hooked. The axioms that undoubtedly jump into your mind, if you have been exposed to any fishing literature at all, are "tight lines" and "don't give him slack!" Slack line will supposedly result in lost fish. I believed this, too, until I was exposed to Lee's stories of making fish "act" for his outdoor films, and anecdotes of his saving big fish in tough situations through the timely use of slack line.

As Lee explains it, a trout or salmon has carefully chosen the spot in which he was lying before he took your fly. He was where he wanted to be. If the hook is set and then slack is given, no feeling of being tethered follows. If no pressure is put on him, he will not run or jump; he will return to his special place. Nothing is pulling on him so why should he go somewhere else? The setting of the hook could be likened to a mosquito bite on a human. You feel it and it is over.

If you don't want to alarm your fish and give him the strategic advantage, use the tactic of giving immediate slack after the hook is set and use the time you'll gain to help things go your way. Reel in the slack line, get in a better position downstream, fold up your wading staff so you won't trip on it as you move around, get your camera around your neck ready to shoot photos of jumps or at release time. Use the time for whatever concerns you.

If you've hooked the fish at the edge of a pool bordered by wild rapids through which you can't follow him, or if there is a brush pile or snag nearby, giving him slack can disarm him and make him feel safe until you can coax him away from such a place with light pressure.

The first time I ever needed to use slack, I needed a lot of time. I had accompanied Lee to Scotland for his appearance in an "American Sportsman" television segment on Atlantic salmon. We were on the River Dee in July, and instead of being damp and rainy as Scotland is supposed to be, the sun had been shining brightly for ten days and the river was low, as was the mood of the very few salmon that seemed to be in it. Lee had caught a fish but it hadn't jumped very much and, in order to make the film better, I was asked to help. While Lee continued to fish with the film crew on hand, a helpful friend, Peter, took me downstream to try my luck. Thirty minutes later I rose a salmon on a hitched fly, but couldn't get him to rise again on the next two or three casts. I took the hitch off and let the fly swim underwater and was rewarded with a strike. As soon as I felt the connection, I lowered the rod and took off all pressure. The fish settled down. Peter took out his walkie talkie, brought along for just this purpose, and radioed upstream to the crew.

The crew was doing a lip synch segment and couldn't be interrupted. They finished, got the word, packed up their gear, piled into two Jeeps and one car and headed downstream. By Peter's watch, it was twenty-two minutes before they came into view. Then the equipment had to be unloaded and set up, cameras had to be carried out into the river, mikes were hooked up again on Lee, to whom I had handed the rod, and his companion, Allan Sharpe. Finally, the word "now" cued Lee to tighten up on my friend *Salmo salar* and begin the playing action.

He was there—after thirty-eight minutes. It certainly made a believer out of me and everyone else on the scene in the value of slack line as a tactic. Luck wasn't with us, though, and the salmon was good for only one jump for the camera before the leader broke and it was traced back to my having cast a wind knot in it . . . shame, shame. (A wind knot is an overhand knot that forms in the leader and reduces the strength of the monofilament at that spot. It is usually caused by imperfect casting but is blamed on the wind because wind makes it

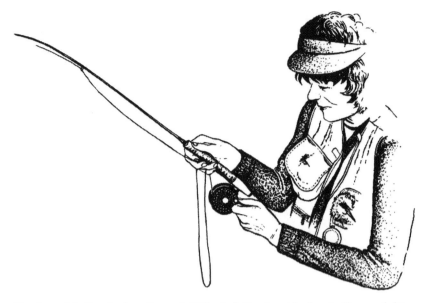

Play large fish directly from the reel. With slack line to get back onto the spool, let the fish take line out from under the middle finger while the pinky guides what's left onto the reel.

more likely to occur. There was no wind that day.)

Slack line is a tactic, not your whole game. It may not work from angles that allow current-flow to act on the slack line; it may not work with barbless hooks, but then again it often does. Think it out in each case, but let me warn you that if you are with a fishing companion or guide who has not become familiar with using slack line when playing a fish, you may be given one hell of a time about it, even if you prove its merits. Old adages die hard.

From the Reel
Once the fish is hooked, brace the rod against the underside of your forearm and decide how you will play him—whether it should be "from the reel" or, if it's a small fish, "by hand." Small trout, those that are 6 to 10 inches long, tend to jump up and down more than they run, so it's likely to be a short, wild, and exciting show—like our cat on the leash. If the line is not too long and you can keep it from catching on anything, just strip the line in. Pass it under the middle finger of your rod hand and strip in from behind it.

For larger fish that are likely to take out more line, play them from the reel. If there is slack line from your retrieve as you fished the fly, you can wind it back on the reel and, at the same time, allow the fish to take out some of that line if necessary. Sounds complicated, I know, but it can be done with the middle and pinky fingers of your rod hand.

The line would have been under your middle finger on the strike. If the fish takes line immediately, let it go out under the middle finger, or, if the fish makes a real surge and you think the fly line may catch on something, use your line hand to control it as it goes out; just cup it to make a loose ring and let the fish have all he wants. If, however, the fish takes less than all of the excess slack, let the middle finger control the line that's going out while you keep reeling in, guiding the slack line back on the reel with your pinky. When all the loose line is back on the reel, the playing really begins.

Keeping the fly line under a finger of your rod hand is very important when playing a fish. You'll feel changes in pressure through your finger before you'll see them in the rod's reaction and you can instantly increase or decrease the part this finger plays.

Now, once he's on the reel, don't just stand there unless it's to

Fly fisher A has pulled her rod back too far (beyond 90°) and it is too wobbly to play the fish properly. Angler B has much more control.

your advantage. Playing a fish well may entail moving around a bit to counteract his actions. He may do the directing for a while, but you are not the one being played. Your tactics will be simple: Never let him rest (unless it's to your advantage, as in using slack). Instead, let him expend his energy running or jumping, but the instant he stops, in that little void of inaction, apply rod pressure to move him toward you, reeling in line as you are able. If he makes a sudden surge, take your hand off the reel and let him go freely, but be ready to reapply the pressure the instant he stops going full bore.

Raise the rod tip when you can move him toward you and, as he keeps coming, lower it again as you reel in the line. This pumping action is used in all types of fishing. Keep the lowering and raising as smooth as you can and never take the rod back beyond a 90-degree angle to an imaginary hard-to-fish line. Farther back will make the rod wobble and, if the pressure is too great, perhaps fracture the rod above the grip.

When a fish takes all of your fly line and you are into the backing, you had better be moving toward him. The drag caused by the thickness and length of the 90 feet of fly line in the water can put great strain on your leader tippet. When a fish runs, a rod held at a high angle increases the drag on the line more than it does at a low angle. If your leader tippet is seemingly light for the weight of the fish, lower your rod a bit when he runs to reduce the strain.

Follow the fish wherever he goes—if you can. This can mean chasing him through rapids downstream and around obstacles such as rocks. Try to keep all tension off the line so that neither line nor leader will abrade against rocks or snags. If the snag is a weed bed, you can use slack as a tactic.

In one of my recent experiences, a beautiful rainbow was lying in plain sight among the weed beds that are typical in certain areas of Montana's Nelson's Spring Creek. My Pale Morning Dun deceived the trout but then he headed straight into the nearest weeds. I lowered the rod to relieve the tension and moved upstream of the snag to take the current's pressure off the fly line. I waited. It seemed like eternity but it was no more than one full minute before he came out the way he went in and I was able to coax him to hand. A joy to behold, he was fat, healthy, and almost iridescent in his rainbow beauty, but my greatest joy was the feeling of confidence the successful slack technique returned to me. I always wonder if it will work after I haven't used it for a long time. Every use increases its value.

When a fly-hooked fish jumps, relax the tension and "bow" to him so there is no tension against which he can pull. If he shakes his head or tries to rub the hook on a rock or the bottom of the stream,

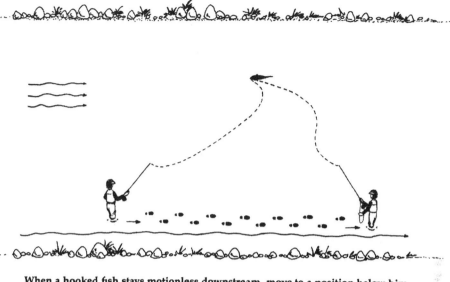

When a hooked fish stays motionless downstream, move to a position below him and add the current's pressure to your steady pull.

give him slack and change your position. If he "sulks," that is, he is downstream of you, positioned in the current so that you can't move him, go below him to apply pressure from this different angle. He can't hold in the current and fight your pressure from below him without tiring. He'll have to move.

Never pull from directly upstream, or when he is facing downstream with the leader over his head or under his belly. The latter circumstance would indicate that you are pulling from the side opposite that on which he is hooked.

A sideward pressure, with the rod close to horizontal, is another tactic to use when the fish is opposite you and stationary. Angle the rod so that the pressure comes to the fish from downstream rather than upstream.

The time to put maximum pressure on a fish to bring him toward you is when neither you nor the fish is moving. Line is not being brought in nor is the fish taking any out. It's called "static" pressure and this is when you'll want to know how much pressure your leader tippet can stand so that you can, if necessary, use it to its maximum strength.

At the beginning of every season, or at least once in your life, you should make up a leader with three feet of 5X for a tippet. Tie the tippet end around a post, the bumper of your car, or some other stationary object. Put a bend in your rod as if you had a fish hooked and see if you can break the tippet with this bent-rod pull. Do not exceed the 90-degree playing angle mentioned earlier.

It is incredible to realize the strength of so light a tippet. It is about 4-pound-test and I doubt that you can break it. Even a 7X leader tippet can be 2-pound test. It will open your eyes and you'll know something ninety-nine out of a hundred fishermen don't: how much pressure the tippet can stand on a straight, hard pull. Try more than one strength of leader so you can compare them. This is the strength you'll call on when playing a fish under the condition of static pressure.

A few words of caution: If you pull at maximum strength too often during the playing, you may enlarge the hook's hole and, if the fish gets slack line at the wrong instant, the fly may fall out. Use the technique wisely. It can make the difference between an overly long fight and one that is perfectly done. The measure of playing a fish well is that it should take no more than one minute per pound from strike to capture.

There is a little-known playing technique called "walking" a fish upstream. I don't know exactly why it works, but it does. It's another bonus technique that can lift your spirits. Occasionally, when you are

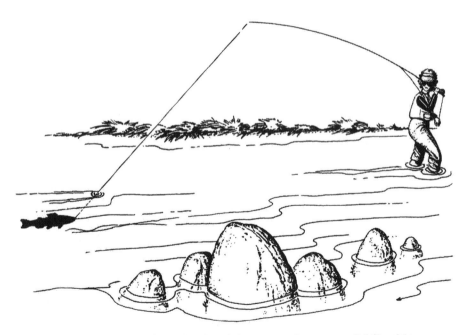

Leading a fish upstream is a helpful tactic in an area where you can't follow him.

playing a big fish and keep moving to a position below him, you suddenly find yourself at the lower end of the pool, beyond which you don't want him to go. There may be rapids, for instance, or very deep water or an impassable shoreline.

Most fish will stop and rest just before they go out of a pool into difficult water, and that's when you start the walking. Hold the rod halfway between vertical and horizontal, put a careful bend in the rod and, pretending you have ball bearings in your knees as you face upstream, start walking as smoothly as you can so there is no jouncing of the rod tip. The fish will follow along like a puppy.

Once you've got him to the head of the pool, resume the playing. It's usually a one-time walk, although in the fall of 1988 an unusually stubborn steelhead on British Columbia's Copper River allowed me to walk him back up the river twice, about seventy-five yards each time.

A fly rod is meant to cushion the shocks of playing the fish, and that's why "tip up" is said so often. The tip bends down with the surges of the action. Your rod action should be such that no matter what the size of the fish, the strain will not be felt too easily in your hand and forearm if you have braced it there. A moderately stiff butt on the rod will serve this purpose. The rod's "backbone" should extend beyond the halfway point in its length so that the fish's weight will not double up the rod and take away your control. For the purpose of playing big fish, look for spring without sogginess when you choose your fly rod.

The Landing

Shallow water and an approaching shoreline are very threatening to the wild creature you have hooked. Everything in his psyche warns him of the dangers of such a place; he will be visible to predator birds and animals. With no place to hide, he'll use all of his strength and courage to resist your efforts. This is when he is most likely to surge away and break off.

Wade out into deeper water, the quietest available, as he is winding down in the contest. Once positioned there, stand still and he will come to accept your legs as tree branches or something else that belongs in the stream. Then you can coax and lead him by using rod pressure from one side angle or another. He may swim in a circle around you and you can plan the actual taking.

When any fish is a rod's length away, he should be ready to quit. This is a time, though, when you want absolutely no drag on your reel; if he makes a last-minute surge, stop reeling and release the rod hand's middle finger instantly or he may break the tippet. More fish are lost at this time in the fight than at any other time through anglers'

When landing a fish, submerge the net, then lead the fish into it headfirst.

carelessness. Don't take anything for granted at this most critical point.

To use a landing net, submerge it downstream. Bring the fish over it headfirst and then lift the net. If a guide is using the landing net, don't turn the responsibility for the landing completely over to him. Ask him to submerge the net and then you bring the fish over it. Don't expect him to "catch" it. A net cannot be moved easily once it is submerged. If you are landing a fish from a boat, don't let the fish get out of your vision (behind the guide, for instance). You must be prepared for that last second's dash for freedom so that you can release tension. The responsibility is yours until the capture is complete.

To take a fish by hand, take a firm hold with a wet hand over his "shoulders," ahead of his dorsal fin (the one on top) and behind his pectoral fins (the forward bottom fins) so his breathing apparatus will not be harmed. Fingers in his gills spell d-e-a-t-h to any game fish.

Atlantic salmon can be tailed by hand, but generally a woman's hand is neither large enough nor strong enough to take the big ones. My hand can't hold more than a 9- or 10-pounder. To tail a fish, grab the "wrist" ahead of the tail with your palm against the body, circling it with your thumb and forefinger upward in a holding position. If you can lift the fish tail first, the pressure of your hold will paralyze him and there won't be any thrashing or twisting to get free. If you can't lift the fish, keep your grip on the tail and pull him backward through the water to shore. Do this only if you plan to keep him, because pulling him backward starts the suffocation process.

If you plan to release the fish, beaching it in shallow water is a good technique for bringing fish in headfirst. You lead or direct them with the rod tip. With small fish you can pull them in; with a larger fish position yourself to get the nose pointed in the right direction, then lead him with the rod tip. A fish can't reverse itself without swimming through a half circle of space. The head pressure exerted on him can keep him from doing this and his own swimming will take him ashore.

Killing Your Fish

A fish you plan to keep should be dispatched as quickly as possible. A decisive rap on top of his head with a sharp rock will do it very well, or you can turn the fish upside down and hit his head on a sharp rock, one that will remain steady during the blow. Some anglers carry "billy clubs" made for this purpose.

I caught my first trout on a fly when I was about twelve years old. I had a wicker creel with ferns in it and I put the 10- or 11-inch rainbow in it carefully, closed the lid, and headed back along the riverbank to show my catch to the rest of the family. Having seen lots of fish lying on ferns in photographs, I presumed this one would just lie still, too. As he started to suffocate he flopped around, and I didn't want to hear it. It made me feel terrible, and yet the idea of killing it on purpose was something I couldn't seem to cope with. A young girl's avoidance of reality, I guess. I ran the rest of the way and Dad did the dirty work, tipping its head backward to break its neck. This is another way to make the kill and it's a clean way on a small fish. After watching Dad, I found myself thinking "I can do that," and I did with my second trout.

Releasing

On a planned release, when I know the fish is mine, a terrible anxiety comes over me to get him unhooked and put back in the water as quickly as possible. I find myself talking to him, saying silly things like "Take it easy, fellow, you'll be free in a minute" and "Okay, okay, hold still now." And on the release, "Go grow a little" or "There, that wasn't so bad, was it?" I feel like a mother sending a child out into the world, worrying about its safety. Mostly, though, I think, "Thank you for taking my fly and letting me see you in all your glory."

There are a few different ways to release trout. If you have taken him in a net, keep it and the fish in the water and he'll come up head-

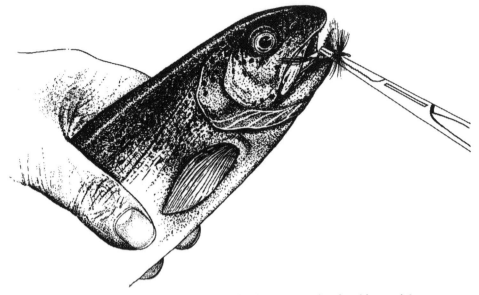

Forceps are helpful for backing out the hook. Use a wet hand and be careful not to put your fingers in the fish's gills as you hold it steady.

first. You can hold him as described earlier, ahead of the dorsal but well behind his gills, while you back the hook out.

If, like mine, your fingers are not always strong enough to take out the hook barehanded, use forceps or fisherman's pliers. They give you much more leverage to do the unhooking quickly. If the fly is deep in the fish's throat, the longer-handled forceps should work. If too much time is going by and you think he is likely to be hurt with more handling, snip the leader as close to the fly as possible and let him go. The hook will rust and dissolve in a week or two, or so I'm told. At least he'll have a chance.

A second method uses the trout's weight to help release the hook. Without touching the fish, take the hook by the bend and lift it out of the water high enough to feel the weight of the fish. Bob it up and down until the fish falls off. You are backing the hook out, with the fish's help.

On a small trout you have a third option. Put your thumb over his lower jaw to keep his mouth open and back the hook out. Because trout have teeth you may get your skin grated, but he'll usually hold still for about twenty to thirty seconds. I recently used this method to release a 16-inch brown for a companion and got a puncture that infected a few days later. A protective thumb stall is the answer.

Barbless hooks make releasing a trout easy. You can buy them barbless or pinch down the barbs on flies you already own.

Because of my sense of urgency on releases, I often fail to measure or examine my fish as closely as I could have. There is a clear, plastic, self-adhesive measuring tape available that can be put on your rod shaft above the grip and makes telling the truth about the size of trout a lot easier. To estimate the weight of salmon, steelhead, or any other large fish you plan to release, measure its length and girth and use this reasonably accurate formula: Multiply the length by the square of the girth, and divide by eight hundred.

If the fish you plan to release is exhausted and he can't swim away on his own, be prepared to revive him. In a stream, if you landed him in quiet water, move out to faster water and hold him loosely, head into the current, until he breathes on his own. There is a common misconception that he should be rocked forward and then backward, but each time you move him backward you are suffocating him. From a boat, or on foot in shallow saltwater, move or walk your fish against any natural current or tide flow.

Catch-and-release is an idea whose time has finally come. When I married Lee, it was his primary conservation cause. He had coined the phrase, "A good game fish is too valuable to be caught only once" in 1936, and finally in 1964 the first catch-and-release area in the country was established in Yellowstone Park. That same year New York State established 4 miles of catch-and-release on the Beaverkill. It is 5.1 miles now, but 3.2 miles have been added on the Willowemoc, a tributary. These no-kill stretches are always full of fish and, in pools such as Cairn's, no matter how many anglers crowd into it, each has a trout to fish for. Many other states throughout the country have no-kill areas and most of the fly anglers I know practice catch-and-release for all species wherever they travel whether the regulations call for it or not.

It is true that some of the fish show signs of having previously been caught, but they are still able to take a fly, still able to feed. I like to think that being caught once a day is like an aerobic exercise period for them; that after the second or third time they come to enjoy the challenge. Lee once suggested to a visiting angler, who was startled to see a trout finning backward beneath his fly, that the fish was not only examining the fly to see who tied it, but was checking out the diameter of the leader tippet to see what his chances would be of breaking off.

Through catch-and-release the trout become smarter, more difficult to deceive, and a greater challenge. When you put them back, they are there for your own or someone else's pleasure on another day. As fly fishing grows in popularity, designating no-kill areas on appropriate streams is one of the ways to ensure that there will be enough fish for the growing number of anglers.

Losing Fish

Not all fish stories have happy endings and you may be more likely to remember the details of the one that got away than of the ones you caught. Losing a fish is a big disappointment, large fish or small, because you don't always know why you lost it. With a clue and a little analytical thinking you may be able to figure out what happened. The silver lining is that you'll learn from the experience, know where something went wrong, and, with a little luck, not have the same experience again. Remember that this is a sport; don't let the frustration of a lost fish grow out of proportion to the overall good time you surely had.

The first clue as to what happened is whether or not you got the fly back. If the fly is still on your leader, chances are that you did nothing wrong; the fish wasn't hooked well. There's not much you can do about that. Relive the playing, however, to figure out if, perhaps, you put too much pressure on the fish (anglers call it "horsing") and enlarged the hook's point of entry. Putting pressure on the fish from the wrong side, as mentioned earlier, could enlarge the hole. Sometimes, though, you get the fly back before the playing has really begun and that's a no-fault, just the way the cookie crumbled.

If the fly stays with the fish, the detective work begins with the end of what's left of the leader. If there is a curl, a knot came untied and you can determine which one by how much of the leader remains. If the leader broke, the end will show a clean cut. So the famous expression "The fish was so big it broke my line" is a hollow excuse. What you are really telling a knowledgeable angler is that one of the following occurred:

1. You were careless in the tying of your knots, at the fly or in your leader.

2. Less than perfect casting put a wind knot in your leader and, under the strain of playing a fish, its 50 percent strength (as opposed to 90 to 95 percent strength in good knots) broke.

3. The stretch in the tippet was used up (perhaps it was too short), and the strength, or pound test, wasn't up to the pressure you put on him; you pulled too hard.

4. You didn't release tension or take off the drag quickly enough when he made a sudden bid for escape.

Angler's fault. Better luck next time!

12

Wading

Wading is an adventure for me. The pressure of the running water against my legs gives me great pleasure, a feeling of being a part of the stream itself. It somehow makes me feel more closely related to the creatures within it, the fish I seek to catch. But if there is any speed to the flow, as soon as the water rises above my crotch the experience is heightened by a hint of danger, the unknown and unexpected. My feet want to come off the bottom. It's the way I'm built.

The ideal wading physique is for the bulk of your body weight to be above the waist, in your shoulders and chest and, therefore, out of the water. My bulk is under the water, in my hips and legs. I don't know the physics of it, but it certainly keeps wading interesting when the flow begins to quicken and the water deepens.

One of the ways to equalize the weight is to carry some in your vest. My husband, Lee, who is slim and tall, feels that by weighting his vest with about fifteen pounds of gear to hold him to the streambed he can better meet a river's wading challenges. Lee has enormous length and breadth to his back; there is no way you or I can carry that much weight comfortably. Instead we must wade with great care.

You know you are in trouble when you can feel the sand or pebbles running out from beneath your boots and your heels rise no matter how hard you try to get them back down. It once happened to me on the Yellowstone River just above Buffalo Ford in the park. We were fishing with friends, guide Bob Jacklin and his dad, Bob Sr. We had enjoyed a good morning catching cutthroats, but my well-worn waders chose that day to self-destruct, and I had to dry out at lunch. It was then that Bob Sr. insisted I borrow his boot-foot waders while he took a siesta. Bob, Lee, and I headed upstream until Bob suggested I cross a small tributary to get to the main river while he and Lee went farther up.

We parted and I started across. The water looked a bit swift and I had a moment of doubt but figured Bob was a good judge. On the third step I felt my muscles start to respond to the quickening flow. Step four made me think I'd better hurry and get through this. Step five brought the water level to just above my knees and the gravel under my feet started to go. The boots were a man's size 9 and were two to three inches longer than my woman's size 8. They had felt okay as we walked upriver on dry land, but now, try as I might, I couldn't get the toes down. I stuck the butt of my fly rod down next to my feet to use as a staff. The rod bent with the current.

I stood there balancing back and forth, waiting to be swept off my feet. Understand that if I had fallen in, the only danger would have been to my dignity. I would have floundered to quieter water and stood up and got on with the fishing, but I had my treasured $200 Rollei 35 in my wader pocket and that was why I had no desire to go in the drink.

I let out a weak "help" to follow the script, never expecting it to be heard by my unseen companions, but, good guide that he was, Bob had hung back to watch me cross and came to my rescue like a young bull moose.

God, what strength in those legs! He got to me quickly but with the force of the water on those big boot feet I couldn't just take his hand and move. He had to grab me bodily and we did a crazy dance, gradually getting over to the quiet water. After we'd finished laughing I noticed that my fly, which had been in the rod's hook keeper, had released itself and was now embedded in Dad Jacklin's wader leg. Sorry, Dad.

I got myself together and Bob crossed back over the tributary and disappeared. A minute later his voice called, "Joan? Did you lose your can of line grease? (yup) It's here in the foot of my boot." Crazy dance, all right. It had popped out of the top pocket of my vest, from under the fly patch flap, into his waders.

The lessons learned:

1. Don't wear anyone else's boots.

2. Do carry a wading staff.

3. Don't think you can cross the same rough water a male companion can cross because he thinks you can.

4. Carry a camera that can be safely immersed in water.

You will have to accept that your tall, male angling companions can wade more deeply than you can. They will have access to fish that you can't reach—no matter how proficient your casting may be. I find it doesn't bother me too much when the river is swift and the bottom slopes quickly. That seems to be a masculine situation, period. But when the slope is gradual and the flow is something I could handle and my husband's eight-inch height advantage lets him wade *fifteen feet* farther than I can and he reaches those salmon on the other side of the current, as happened on Norway's Gaula River, I vow to come back in my next life as a tall, broad-shouldered, slim-hipped male angler. I cast my heart out in that session and was always five to ten feet short. Lee hooked and landed a 23-pounder in the first five minutes.

Footwork

Wading is slower than you think it ought to be and the footwork, in difficult water, is similar to a shuffle. To wade safely, move your feet so that they skim the bottom rather than lifting them up and putting them down as you do on land. Move one foot forward only as far as your back foot can sustain your balance, then, moving your back foot just above the bottom, bring it to meet the other.

Here are things to remember when wading:

1. Never move one foot unless the other is securely placed.

2. After you enter the water, look ahead to where you will move your forward foot but, as you move it, don't look down. You may get vertigo. Focus instead on another spot farther away.

3. When you cross a stream with a strong current, do it on the diagonal, so that the force is pushing you in the direction you

want to go. This is the easiest way to cross, even in a gentle current.

4. When you get the first hint of trouble, don't go any farther; you may just get yourself into more trouble. Go back the way you came and try another approach.

5. Stand sideward to the current to fish so that you have a thin silhouette broaching the current (the width of one leg) instead of a broad one (the width of two legs).

6. Very clear water may be deeper than it looks.

7. Large, flat-surfaced rocks are more slippery than smaller ones.

8. Know your limitations.

For the adventurous: In water at waist level or above, you can lean back against the flow and take your feet slightly off the bottom, both at one time, to move downstream, instead of having to reach out with one leg, which would make you vulnerable to the full force of the water. In spite of the way I'm built, I once found myself in water in which I could try this. It worked. I'm still looking for the second place.

If you are the least bit fearful of wading, forget about catching fish and leave your rod on the bank. Take a wading staff and explore the area you want to fish until your fears are dissipated.

Wading Staffs

A wading staff is a bit of insurance. I would never try to wade with a staff anywhere I was sure I couldn't wade without one. It's like a third leg, but it's not a replacement for the other two. It is valuable in marginal situations, perhaps when there is a little extra speed to the current or when you need to move only a few more feet to reach that wonderful fishing spot. In unfamiliar water it can help you find the edges of a gravel-bar path, an area of soft bottom, or a large rock in your way.

A one-piece staff may be stronger and therefore more reliable than a folding staff, but you always have to be aware of where it is, and it can easily get in your way when you're actually fishing.

A folding staff can remain in its holder or somewhere in your vest until you need it and be folded back in when you don't. The famous Folstaff, which is made of sections of aluminum tubing around an

Joining forces with another angler is a great way to get across water that is difficult to wade. Hold upper arms and walk diagonally downstream.

elastic rope, was developed by its designer, Arthur Stoliar, for his fishing wife, Joan. It is a "couple" project and, as of this writing, Arthur and Joan still put Folstaffs together evenings while listening to classical music.

If you must cross a stream that makes you anxious and you know that it will take all of your skill and strength, and you have a companion at hand, male or female, there's a way of coupling that makes it a snap. Just entwine your arms, left and right or right and left, holding each other's upper arms. Put the stronger wader on the upstream side. Crossing in this manner is like "walking on water" if your companion is a tall, strong man, but even if it's just another you, physically, it really helps. Don't forget to slant downstream if it's rough going.

Falling In

There are a lot of horror stories about the dangers of falling in without a belt on your waders. The belt supposedly keeps the water out and the air in, to keep you from being sucked under. It doesn't work that way. Water will still get below the belt, maybe a bit more slowly if the belt is pulled very tight. But water won't "suck you down" because water doesn't weigh anything underwater. The only time water in your waders is a handicap is when you try to get out of the stream; then it can be real trouble. Therefore, think about how to get out of the waders before you must get out of the water.

In the 1950s, at the height of talk about the dangers of falling in while wearing chest waders, Lee decided to prove it or disprove it for himself and the angling public. With a photographer present, he dove off a bridge into Vermont's Battenkill River wearing boot-foot waders and no belt. The photograph of him in midjump has become rather famous. The waders didn't give him any trouble; the sweater he was wearing to ward off the October chill did. It was difficult for him to get his arms out of the water to swim ashore, but he made it. The things that are most dangerous are those that are the least expected, whether in the river itself, such as hitting your head on a rock, or in your clothing and gear.

If you have any misgivings about waders and safety, do your own experimenting in safe circumstances. Submerge yourself in waders in water chosen carefully. There should be some depth and some current, but no dangerous rocks or whirlpools. Even a swimming pool would teach you something! Have a companion with a life-saving rope in case of the unexpected.

It's the unknown that generates panic, and panic is thought to be the greatest contributing factor to wading deaths. If you do fall and are swept downstream, try to get your feet downstream of your body, reaching down whenever possible to find the bottom shallowing. Once you touch bottom you have a chance.

There are lesser incidents that happen to all of us. It's easy to trip or slip when you are wading if you move too fast and a rock rolls under your foot. I finally bought a "fishing watch," one that can take submersion, and this, along with my waterproof camera, has allowed me to fall in with less worry. The problem then becomes one of lost dignity. The first thing you do when you are back on your feet is look around to see who was watching.

Wading Gear

The weight and bulk of chest waders is another of the subtle things that has kept women from stream and river fishing. When I started to fish in the 1930s, chest waders were made of rubber and canvas and available in men's sizes. I thought of them as cumbersome death traps. No way would I have entered a river wearing something like that. I was able to fit into a boy's size hip boot and so my trout fishing was limited to hip boot-depth water. I missed a lot.

It wasn't until 1978 that Uniroyal's Red Ball Division revolutionized the wader market by introducing flyweights: stocking-foot, nylon chest waders coated with polyurethane. Weight, three ounces; size, unisex. They took the fly-fishing field by storm. I felt lucky to have lived long enough to witness their development, and I've been in flyweights ever since. You can dance in them; you can drive in them. I once went into our country bank, on a fishing lunch break from the Beaverkill, before I realized I was still wearing them. The fit is a bit loose, because of the need to bend your knees as you climb up and down riverbanks, but with a belt, vest, and scarf, it's easy to look feminine while wearing them.

Stocking-foot Chest Waders

The original is the three-ounce nylon made by Red Ball. Other manu-

Clockwise from left: flyweights with belt, hippers, neoprenes, wading shoe.

facturers now do this wader with slightly thicker material for more durability. Check them out and be sure they are, in fact, light and flexible. The stocking-foot makes them a little like Dr. Denton kid's pajamas, so you must have separate shoes.

A cotton, wool, or neoprene wading sock worn between wader and shoe helps to keep the bottom of the wader from abrading as a result of the gravel that may get inside the shoes in stream conditions.

There is absolutely no insulating quality to these lightweights, so you must wear underneath anything necessary to keep you warm.

Neoprene Form-fitting Chest Waders

These waders are the closest we come, in fly fishing, to the stretch pants of the ski slopes. Developed for scuba diving, neoprenes are warm, cozy, and flexible. There is nothing better for cold-water wear. A little extra time must be spent in putting them on, and between wearings they must be turned inside out to dry the slight condensation that occurs, but they are worth the trouble in the early or late trout season, and on salmon and steelhead rivers anytime the water or air temperature is low enough to cause discomfort.

If you own both flyweights and neoprenes, you will need only one pair of wading shoes.

Hip Boots

In hot weather and in low water, hip boots fill the bill. Crotch-high, they attach to your belt with loops. Once the water nears midthigh level, however, your chances of getting wet are 99 percent as you move through the water on an irregular stream bottom.

Stocking-foot "hippers" in the flyweight category can fill out your needs for a complete system. You can use the same wading shoes as you do with your chest waders.

Traditional hip boots are one piece with boot feet and are available in rubber, canvas, and neoprene, or with one material for the foot and a different one for the leg.

Wading Shoes

Worn for wading wet or over stocking-foot waders, wading shoes are made of canvas, leather, or artificial materials. They are available with either laces for good ankle support or Velcro closings for ease. Wading shoes in women's sizes are still not found universally, but some do exist. Naturally, it is the smaller sizes that are the most difficult to find. All wading shoes are made to accommodate a heavy sock or neoprene bootie between the stocking foot and wading shoe, and you can adjust the thickness of that layer to get a proper fit.

Felt Soles

Felt soles are a must on shoes or boots. These help to keep you from slipping on smooth or algae-covered rocks. You can go a step farther and get sandals or rubbers with aluminum cleats to wear over your felt soles for really dangerous and unusually slippery conditions.

13

Clothing and Gear for Stream Fishing

Ore of the attractions of wading a stream is that you become a part of the world of the trout, salmon, or steelhead that you seek. Carry this thought when you select clothing color because you will want to blend in with your surroundings. Dark-colored waders match the color of underwater debris. In your upper-body clothing, avoid colors such as hot orange or fuschia. Instead, choose blue, green, khaki, taupe, and gray, which are less likely to spook fish in the arm movements of casting. Color choice is mostly common sense, and you do have the latitude on big rivers, where you are never close to the fish, to wear anything you want. The smaller the stream and the clearer the water, the more important your choice of color or its intensity. A fish's vision as it affects us is upward and outward.

You can retain your personality and dress well as an angler. Vests and waders are available in several colors and a scarf can add any other touch you need.

Garb for All Weathers
Heat . . . cold . . . sun . . . rain . . . these are the elements fishermen

come to know intimately. Layered clothing is the best solution to the changing conditions you may encounter in a day of fishing or on a trip where you are not quite sure of what to expect. Think about the following options.

When experiencing heat, consider donning a lightweight cotton shirt, lightweight or mesh vest, or some kind of simple pocket-pack on a belt. Use flyweight waders or hip boots, or, in extremely hot weather, wade wet with felt-soled wading shoes.

When the temperatures are cold, layering needs to be more seriously planned. Expand your wardrobe so that it includes polypropylene underwear, which comes in light, medium, or heavy weight; turtlenecks; a cotton or wool sweater (which should always be covered by a windbreaker because hooks catch in exposed sweaters); a down jacket; and a head-hugging knit hat, such as a navy-watch style. On your hands use fingerless wool gloves, or, better yet, neoprene gloves that are fully fingered but have slits through which you can poke fingers when you need to tie knots. Wool socks or two-layer Bama sockettes worn over light socks will insulate your feet.

When the wind is howling, wear a windbreaker and/or rain jacket with a hood. If you prefer a hat to a hood, use one with a narrow or medium-wide brim or bill. Too wide a brim will be caught by the wind. It is tough for a woman to keep a hat on her head in windy conditions because of the bulk of our hair. A tie cord is a must. If there is none with your hat, use cording or monofilament to make your own. If my hat still refuses to stay on, I put my windbreaker or rain jacket hood over the hat, leaving the bill sticking out, and tie it securely under my chin.

Protection from the harmful rays of the sun is important and the obvious costume will include a long-sleeved shirt and a brimmed hat, perhaps with side and back flaps. I find a visor less warm. Don't forget sunscreen and Polaroid sunglasses.

Polaroids are necessary for fly fishing. They cut much of the glare that would otherwise keep you from seeing below the water's surface. Both wading and seeing fish will be easier. You will be handicapped without them. Polaroids are available over the counter with glass or plastic lenses in all shapes and sizes, from wraparounds to bifocals. Your optician can fix you up with prescription Polaroids. In either case, choose glasses with sideplates, if they are available, to cut out peripheral glare.

You may encounter a problem with the weight and size of most fishing Polaroids, as I have. They will slip down your nose, especially if you are wearing sunscreen; this kills your concentration. You may need a retainer such as Croakies or Spec-Socs to keep large glasses in place, but keep looking for a lightweight pair. I am currently wearing the Floater Polaroids, which weigh less than one ounce, offer 100 percent ultraviolet protection, and will float if you lose them, providing you don't have nonfloatable straps on them. They are available from Eyeglasses International in San Francisco. Because they have plastic lenses, which scratch more easily than glass lenses, and are relatively inexpensive, they may have to be replaced fairly often. Fisherman Eyewear in Hollister, California, offers a diversity of models, and other companies are entering the fly-fishing market.

When it is raining you will need a hooded rain jacket and a hat with a bill. Choose a "wading" rain jacket, which is short and nonbulky to fit in your vest's back compartment. It should have sealed seams. Wear it over your vest when you need it. A billed hat is worn under your rain hood. This keeps the rain off your face and gives you more freedom to move your head within the hood.

Fly-fishing Vests

Most vests are marketed for men, with the focus on the number of pockets they contain. With their broad backs and large chests, men have plenty of body room for an array of chock-full pockets. Not so for us. We need fewer pockets and must fill them carefully so our breasts will not be uncomfortable from bulk or jabbed by sharp edges.

Keep all the bulky boxes and items in the outside pockets and use the inside pockets for leaders and tippet spools, licenses, and other flat things. Another area to think about is between your armpit and your waist. A filled pocket near the side seams should not force your upper arm outward from your body, either while casting or while fishing the fly.

Because women vary so much in neck-to-waist length and bosom size, I can't give a blanket description of which vest will suit you. Choose carefully, that's all. Large-chested women have the hardest time finding something perfect and often must buy a man's vest.

Buy your vest in a size that is large enough to fit over cold-weather clothing unless you can afford two vests, the second one for light clothing. Decide if you want a short vest or a long vest and use a mirror to help make the decision on the other points of style. Take along some fly boxes and fit them in the pockets. You can look like Santa or Jane Fonda.

There is a subtle impression, given by pockets that sag when they have fly boxes in them, of sagging breasts. This may sound farfetched, but that's what a mirror is for. The fly patch is at breast height or just above, which is good, but don't fill the pocket beneath it too full. The patch on the other side may be two pockets, one outside the other, or it may be one with a divider. One or the other may be more flattering to you.

If you want something other than a vest, the market is expanding steadily. Belt packs and strapped bags and boxes are available in various sizes and colors. Or use your ingenuity.

On a hot July day, Lee's daughter-in-law, Ginger McGuffie, has been seen wearing a big smile and a fly patch pinned to her bikini top while Atlantic salmon fishing in flyweights. The wader pocket holds her clippers and replacement leader. All her flies are in the patch. With a guide to net her fish, she is unencumbered.

Vest Contents

You will need fly boxes, organized by the character of the fly, such as dries, wets, and nymphs, or further by classes of aquatic insects such as caddis, mayflies, and stoneflies. Perhaps you'll carry a separate box for terrestrials: ants, grasshoppers, beetles. And another small box for midges in #18 to #24, and yet another box for leeches, big muddlers, and big stonefly nymphs.

A trout vest is like a woman's purse in that its contents must take care of all needs and emergencies. Here is a list of items for possible inclusion:

Ready-made leaders, and spools of tippet material to modify or repair them
Split shot or wraparound weight to put on your leaders
Strike indicators
Hook sharpener
Clippers for trimming knots
Scissors for trimming knots and/or trimming flies to change their shape
Magic marker to darken light-colored flies
Fly flotant
Forceps for releasing small to medium-size trout
Fisherman's pliers for heavier jobs (pliers can also be used to mash the barb on your hook)
Magnifying eyeglasses; determine the magnification at the time of purchase by tying a #22 fly to a piece of 6X leader material
Polaroids
Thermometer to read stream temperature
Fisherman's gooseneck flashlight (no hands needed)
Safety pin or commercial clipper with a needlelike protrusion to clear the lacquer-filled eye of a hook
Folding staff

Folding insect-catching net
Rain jacket
Insect repellent
Sunscreen
Lipstick and mirror
Camera

My vest includes a small spiral notebook and a pen for notes about one thing or another and a folding Bob Lane drinking cup. This is made of two slabs of stainless steel; it holds a streamside cup of wine nicely, and folds flat. (Mine came from L. L. Bean.) And my "fishing candies" are La Vosgienne Bonbons Fruits, which are delicious drops of flavor in a round metal box.

Some anglers carry extra reel spools with an alternative fly line category (sinking or sink tip). Lee carries an extra reel in the back of his vest when we go on trips, but that's too much bulk for me. I leave my extra reel in the car or in the closest safe place to the fishing.

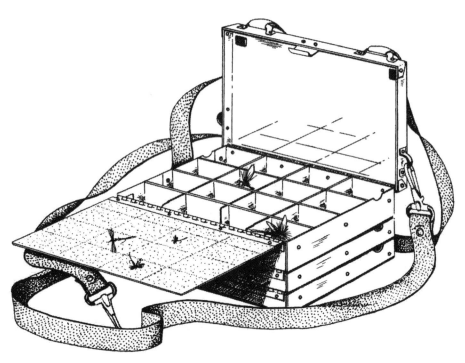

A three-layer chest box can replace a dozen individual fly boxes.

You may want to pare the bulk of your vest, and one way to do so is to use an alternative to individual fly boxes. My upper body is relatively small, and I like to carry lots of trout flies, so I am happily using a Richardson Chest Box (Osceola Mills, PA 16666). A chest box rides in the center of your chest on the upper half of your breasts. The dimensions of my box are 6¼ inches wide by 5¼ inches deep by 2⅞ inches high. It has straps that go over my shoulders, cross in the back, and clip onto each side of the box after passing under my arms.

The chest box is completely comfortable, even for one of my bigger-bosomed friends, and is very convenient. It contains three layers. The top is deepest for dry flies (divided into sixteen compartments), the second compartmented layer is shallower for wets and nymphs, and the third has no sectioning and can be used for leaders, streamers, and so on. On one side of the box is a cylinder-shaped holder for my gooseneck flashlight. The box is made of aluminum, by hand. There are plastic-box systems similar in concept advertised in fly-fishing catalogs and magazines.

I still use a vest with this system. I need it to hold some of the many necessities listed above. I even carry one or two small boxes of flies because, even though the chest box may be full, I don't dare leave these others at home.

The one thing you don't need to carry on the stream is fly-tying material. If you haven't got the fly, how would you possibly have known you were going to need it and brought exactly the right materials? Tying on the stream makes a nice story or film, but forget it otherwise! Tie your flies at home, or in camp; otherwise you'll need a pack-horse to carry all the fly-tying material you might possibly need. With a good selection of both naturals and attractors, plus scissors and a magic marker, you have a good chance of coming up with something that will work, if you present the fly well. And you won't have to leave the action.

14

Ethics and Integrity

*I charge and require you in the name of all noble men that
you do not fish in any poor man's private water . . . without
his permission and good will. . . . Also, I charge you, that
you break no man's hedges in going about your sports, nor
open any man's gates without shutting them again. Also,
you must not use this aforesaid artful sport for covetousness, merely for the increasing or saving of your money,
but mainly for your enjoyment and to procure the health of
your body and, more especially, of your soul. For when you
intend to go to your amusements in fishing, you will not
want very many persons with you, who might hinder you
in your pastime.*

The people with whom you share fishing must be special. It has
long been my belief that if you can fish comfortably with a companion,
you can live with him (not that you'll want to live with everyone with
whom you can fish comfortably). The fishing relationship is one that
includes lots of give and take, but there are parameters. Each person

needs a certain amount of privacy for the total immersion of himself into the fishing experience; he or she needs total concentration and oneness with the surroundings. It's not a place for idle chatter.

The exception is when you are new to the sport. Then a companion will baby-sit you at the beginning of your outing by helping to determine which water you should fish, explaining what might be going on with the insect life, and suggesting the character and size of the fly with which you should begin. Then perhaps he or she will fish near you for a while, stop fishing if you hook one, share in your excitement in playing and landing it, and maybe even take a photograph of your first catch.

The next step is when you and your more knowledgeable companion split up. Alone you may find that success is harder to come by; nothing works; no fish are showing and none are taking your fly. You have exhausted all of the techniques you know and are filled with doubt as to your destiny as a fisherman. You are sure your companion knows why you are not catching anything and forgot to tell you something you should know. Should you interrupt your friend's fishing time with your problems?

It would be considerate to find the friend and, making sure there's been time for the total immersion, watch him or her fish until the time seems right for an interruption. The companion may not be able to solve your problem. It is difficult for one person to fish through another at the same time he himself is fishing. You are always analyzing your own set of conditions; you can't imagine someone else's. Most companions, however, will do their best to help. Then you should go off to do your best, checking back again after more immersion time has passed.

Sharing Space and Time

On a trout stream there may be enough good areas so that you can split up and meet later, but if you must share the same pool, you can do it with one taking the head and the other the tail. If one of you hooks a fish in a relatively small pool, it is considerate for the other to reel in his line to free the area for the playing.

If you have paid money to fish on an Atlantic salmon river or a European trout river, you will probably have been assigned a "beat," the limited area in which you may fish. One of you can start at the top of the beat and the other can start halfway down if you have purchased two "rods." You might have purchased just one rod, which means you cannot fish at the same time and so you must figure an equitable way to share the fishing. Do it by time. Thirty minutes is a good length. When Lee and I are in this situation, we do not count playing time beyond the thirty minutes. One gives that time to the other and the next thirty minutes begins when the fish is lost or landed. If we will be on a river for several days, we take turns as to who starts each day. Neither of us expects extra time because of our sex or our age. This is a sign of maturity in fishing companionship.

Why not share the fishing by counting fish? One person fishes until he catches one, then it's the other person's turn? Worst case scenario: The better or luckiest fisherman catches one in the first five minutes of the day and the second person doesn't catch any for a couple of hours or even all day. Remember, to most anglers, it's the fishing time that's precious, even more than the catching time.

For some kinds of boat fishing, such as floating a river, two people can often fish at the same time. Fly lines, however, are likely to tangle given half a chance to do so, so the distance between you, along with the direction and velocity of the wind, will determine if it will work.

When two people can fish at the same time in a moving boat, the person in front will be getting first crack at the fish. Change positions every hour or half-hour to share this advantage. If there isn't room for two people to fly cast, another way to share it is for the angler in the bow to use a fly rod while the angler in the stern uses a spinning or bait-casting rod. Again, rotate in a prearranged time period, changing tackle as you change position. Lee and I do this when fishing on lakes with a guide for bass, bluegills, or freshwater stripers.

On Atlantic salmon rivers, especially in the early season, the rivers are high and fishing is done from a canoe. The system that has developed over the years for covering the water is for the fishing to be done in "drops." The canoe is anchored in the best spot and the fisherman covers the water in the standard wet-fly pattern of quartering downstream swings. Then the anchor is lifted and the boat is drifted downstream to the next drop. Anglers take turns, changing on each drop. At the best holding places for salmon, the guide may suggest that both of you fish the same drop, just to show the salmon a different fly. Companions take turns as to who begins each day, as mentioned earlier.

In flats fishing from a boat for bonefish, permit, or tarpon, only one person can fish at a time because stalking is involved. You cast only after you have seen your quarry. Time intervals are the solution and, once again, playing time beyond the thirty-minute period doesn't count. Tarpon are a little different. Forty-five minutes playing time is about the minimum for a fish topping 100 pounds and an unskilled fisherman can take hours to land one. Your rules may have to be flexible.

These "rules" are suggestions; the ones you make up may be better, but do make them. Any rules are better than no rules, like the old adage "Good fences good neighbors make." You can change them in the middle of the game if things are too one-sided, as when one angler catches all the fish. It's just that your relationship will not be stretched if you share time equitably.

Lee and I have been fishing together since 1966 and our give and take is pretty easy by now. Because we not only love each other but like each other, we can give the gift of "time." Once we were on the flats at Boca Paila, on Mexico's Yucatan Peninsula. I had the first turn of the morning and I was about three minutes away from the end of it (Lee always lets me know), when a school of permit dimpled the absolutely dead calm surface ahead of us. The telltale dorsal fins looked like scythes when they broke the water at a distance that was a bit too far for me to cast. As the boat neared them I was able to present the fly only twice, with no takes, before my time ran out. I offered the rod to Lee and he said, "Go ahead." Ahhhh, thank you, love. Permit are one of my favorite fish and he knew it. I hooked and landed my second permit on a fly from that school, and he will always have a share in my memory of it.

Sharing Public Water

It used to be that a trout stream was a place to seek solace, away from other people, away from the noise of civilization. It was a place to meditate, listen to the songs of birds, and perhaps see a mink or a fox as you matched wits with wild trout.

If you could see, and perhaps you have, Cairn's Pool on the Beaverkill in New York's Catskill Mountains, you would find the opposite situation: It is formed below the abutments of a Route 17 overpass, and the sounds of traffic can be heard above the soft rush of the river. Parked cars line the old highway along the river, and anglers stand within ten to fifteen feet of each other to fish, in what might appear, to a nonfisherman, to be a new form of group therapy. Cairn's is the most famous pool on the river and at the height of the trout season offers proof that catch-and-release can change what a fisherman seeks in his sport.

Of course, anglers congregate here because there are always plenty of trout in this pool, enough to make it worthwhile to put up with the crowd. Each person has at least one fish to target. There is some jockeying for position, but amazingly, the system works. Although it is first come, first served, there always seems to be room for one more if a trout is rising and no one is working on it.

In a different situation, that of finding one fisherman already in a pool you would like to fish, it is most considerate to fish behind him if he is halfway through it. You would thus be fishing through the water he has already covered. Or, if he is at one end, fish the opposite end.

On the other hand, if you are there first and an angler comes in to fish ahead of you, close enough to keep you from fishing effectively, speak up immediately. You can say, "I beg your pardon?" or something similar to get his or her attention.

Conversations with other anglers, when they are taking a rest from the action, give you a chance to compare notes about fly selection ("I've been using a #22 Blue-Winged Olive and have only caught a few, what about you?"), leader tippet size ("Have you had to use anything smaller than 5X this morning?"), and what's happening in other sections of the river. You'll never know, however, if the answer is the truth, the whole truth, and nothing but the truth. There is some substance to the stories about fishermen's lies. Giving away your edge, even during loose competition, isn't in every fisherman's makeup.

The husband of a woman angler told me this story. They were fishing in an area known for its selective trout in the West Branch of the Delaware. His wife was catching fish, but two anglers whom they had met in the local diner at breakfast were fishing nearby unsuccessfully. The two kept moving closer to see what fly she was using. Finally one of them could stand it no longer and called over to ask. She answered him truthfully. "Oh, come on now," the angler said, "tell us the truth. We know for a fact that fly never works in this part of the river!"

Then there is the male angler who will tell a woman angler which deadly fly he's using when he wouldn't tell another man. My friend Susan Waterfall, fishing with a group of five men on an unfamiliar western river, asked each one for their recommendation. She got five different answers and the five flies. Using them all, she outfished every member of the group.

So there are games within games in the fly-fishing world, but it's all fun if you remember to keep it that way.

Our Integrity

On Atlantic salmon rivers, when anglers fish from a boat, I've often seen guides take over for a woman angler when she cannot cast far enough to cover all the water within a drop. He hooks the fish, she plays and lands it, and back at the lodge it is entered in the log as her catch. I take exception to this. It is neither his catch nor hers, for the record. If it gives the angler pleasure to do it this way, I can understand that, but leave it out of the book, or put both names in it so that other anglers, reading this record, will not be misled. And yes, of course, this practice began with and is still true of some male anglers with the same kind of casting problems.

On the other hand, I've been with salmon anglers of both sexes who could not finish out the drop as well as they wished but would continue to cast within their range, sometimes "puddling" the line cast after cast, but letting the river's current straighten it out, and suddenly they are into a salmon! (Where the guide has chosen to position the boat has a great deal to do with it.) I really respect these fishermen. They are in the sport for more than a fish's weight next to their names in a log book. You will only get better at casting, hooking, and playing through practice. Don't give your precious fishing time to someone else; you can't get it back.

There is a further extension to the two-person catch. It is an insidious thing. People become suspicious of catches claimed by women. Did she or didn't she? Even I have found myself wondering if the unknown woman who is introduced as having made a spectacular catch really made it alone. And then I've been on the other end. I've seen suspicion turn toward me. Many people presumed that I had never fished before I married Lee Wulff, and I had to prove myself over and over again in our early years together.

I did once allow a photo to be taken with a large trout a friend had caught. He wanted to use the picture in a story he was writing. He didn't say I had caught the fish but it was presumed, certainly. Every time I come across my copy of that photo I find myself explaining, to no one, that I didn't catch it. I regret having allowed it and have never let it happen again.

Because female anglers are a minority, the eyes of the fly-fishing community are on us and, in a sense, we have to prove ourselves. By maintaining our integrity we can walk with pride among all anglers.

As the late John Houseman, who represented a financial institution in television commercials, might have put it: "Respect is not given, it must be earned." And what a wonderful, valuable thing it is!

15

Guides

A good guide has the combined attributes of teacher, father, and lover. He'll teach you his techniques, console you when something goes awry, and be as happy as you are when you catch a fish. He'll wait on you, watch out for your safety, and act as if there is no place on earth he'd rather be than right there with you. He'll boost your spirits and help you hit the highs if you are up to it. You are a team!

Good guides know "their" water in flood conditions and drought and they know the lies of the fish throughout the year. They know which flies are currently hot and the best techniques for presenting them, all of which they will share with you once they know you are receptive to the information. On the other hand, if you are a knowing angler, a good guide will respect you and hold back until you ask for his help. You can set the tone in the first five or ten minutes of meeting. Let him know in which areas you would like his advice or help and in which areas you'd like to rely on yourself. Ask pertinent questions to draw out his knowledge. An attitude of mutual respect is key to enjoyable fishing.

A good guide will stand near you, his eyes constantly on the fly.

He is, in effect, fishing through you, which is the essence of good guiding. The more limited your capabilities, the greater his challenge. Lee Marshall of Quebec's Upsalquitch River is one such guide, the first who made me aware of what "good" really was. He was markedly different from those I had met before: guides who would put you in the best place to fish and then go sit on the bank or snooze in the back of the canoe.

The number of good guides is growing. This intensity of purpose is now the hallmark of a breed of young men, and a growing number of women, who are making guiding a profession, rather than using it as something to fill in time until some "productive" work comes along. A guide's forty- to sixty-hour work week is spent on the water and he knows it like the back of his hand. He knows the resident fish and will see things that you may miss, such as the flash of a fish that doesn't break the surface, a rise that is outside your peripheral vision, or the take of a trout in glare conditions.

Tony Cooper was guiding me on Montana's Bighorn River one afternoon under conditions that were terribly difficult for me. It was overcast, gray, and dull, and we were fishing windswept shallow riffles. The wind was blowing opposite the water's flow and the glare made the #22 Adams invisible to me 90 percent of the time even though I knew it was landing approximately where I was aiming it. The browns were there in numbers, but they barely broke the surface, and just sipped in the fly. I felt blind; my contact lenses were about to pop out from the eye strain, and I was getting a headache. Tony was focused on every cast and he'd say "Strike!" Sometimes I'd connect, but I wasn't happy having to depend on him.

Finally, sensing my frustration, he suggested I put a strike indicator on my leader, a half-inch-long piece of Blaze Orange foam, to help me spot the takes. The very thought of using artificial help *on a dry fly* when he didn't need any bruised my ego. Never having done it, though, I wanted the experience. Even the indicator lost its fluorescence in those light conditions, but I did catch a few fish that way and learned something new in the process, thanks to my very able guide.

The experience also offered a challenge I may be able to meet next time. I used to think that if I wasn't born with the skill to see fish as easily as my companions, it was just too bad. Now I know from years of fishing experience that if it can be seen, I can eventually learn to see it, subtle as it may be. You can learn to see in ways you have never seen before once you analyze what you are looking *at*, and know what you are looking *for*. I find that to be really exciting.

A good guide doesn't expect to fish along with you or in place of you. If you choose to alter that arrangement, so be it, but never feel guilty about not letting him fish. You are paying him to do a job; it's your vacation. I was once happily surprised to have steelhead guide Keith Douglas ask to take my rod to put on a hookless fly in order to demonstrate the speed at which the fly was to be waked across the surface. He didn't want to take a fish I could have taken. That is professional.

As I get older I sometimes have to move into high gear to keep up with a young guide as he strides through the woods or along the streambed over rocks that seem to be arranged conveniently for his size 12 shoes rather than my size 8s. Once, on the upper reaches of the Copper River in British Columbia, guide Bob Hull suggested "Since there's not enough room for both you and Lee to fish in this pool, would you like to go exploring upriver?" "Sure," said I. We took off and I found myself having to go at breakneck speed, barely keeping up on the boulder-strewn edges of the streambed. A light suddenly lit up the dim recesses of my brain, and I stopped him. "How long is your inseam?" I asked breathlessly. Startled, he replied, "Thirty-seven inches, why?" "Because mine is twenty-nine," I said. He gave me a big grin and took off again, more slowly.

I hate to bring up the subject of bad guides. You'll know them when you see them. Basically they are lazy, physically and mentally, just like other lazy people you know. They'll sit on the bank until you call them (if you do), or there's a fish to land, or it's lunch time. I've heard of some guides who not only fished along with clients, without asking, but fished ahead of them in the best places. Their attitude implies that you do your thing and they'll do theirs and don't forget to tip.

If you do get stuck with a bad guide, you can muddle through a day as long as he keeps you out of danger and doesn't expect to fish. And, of course you wouldn't hire him again. It's not always a situation with an easy solution, particularly if you have engaged this guide for several days or are at a camp where he has been assigned to you—but taking the initiative may improve the situation.

The best time to prevent the problem is when you make your initial contact with a new guide, which might be by phone. Find out what to expect. How many hours will you fish and are they the best fishing hours? Who provides the lunch and transportation? Does he expect to fish? (Set him straight.) What if it rains or the wind blows too hard to fly fish? Don't be bashful or intimidated. Be direct and straightforward. He'll respect you for it and there will be no surprises.

Occasionally you will meet a woman guide. The western United States has the highest proportion of female guides but, overall, the percentage is still quite small. Guiding is a physically demanding job especially where boats are involved. In the 1940s there were two famous women guides in the Florida Keys: Frankie Albright (married to guide Jimmy) and Bonnie Smith (married to guide Bill), and they were sisters. Fishing out of Islamorada, Frankie guided internationally known angler and trout-fishing authority George LaBranche to his first fly-caught bonefish. Bonnie guided world-renowned angler Joe Brooks to his first permit in May of 1950.

In the mid-1980s, I spent a day fishing with Key West guide Linda Drake (married to guide Gilbert) and, strangely, ended up with laryngitis! We had a wonderful time talking, which I had never done to such an extent with a male guide, as well as fishing. I can only guess that the fairly strong wind, which made seeing the permit difficult, was also the cause of my vocal cord distress.

Linda started guiding at the age of thirty-three and on that day, three years later, was still in love with the job. She told me of her doubts in the beginning, of how critical she is of herself, of the job's rewards. Although she loves to fish, guiding others introduces a "new intrigue out there on the flats." She loves the competition with the fish and the satisfaction of putting people on fish she has outguessed.

A young woman who once thought that the sun rose at 10 A.M., Linda now gets up at 5:30 and does her thirty-minute aerobic workout before the fishing day begins to keep in shape for poling her 16-foot Dolphin. The constant meeting of new people and contact with old-friend clients can generate quite a social life, but she restricts it in the busy season and is in bed by 8 P.M.

Idaho is home for the Drakes in the off-season, where they hunt and fish for fun. No more downhill skiing for Linda, though; she cannot risk an injury that would keep her from guiding the following winter. She is surely a member of the new breed!

[*Editor's note:* Linda hung up her pole after the 1990 season.]

16

Warm-water Fishing: Bass, Panfish, Pickerel, and Pike

Fly-rod bass fishing is the genesis of my being a fisherman, as I related in the Introduction. My dad loved it. Mom didn't fish, so she rowed the boat. From that evening in the early 1930s when my child's mind formed the thought "It is better to be the fisherman than the rower," I shared that love with my late dad.

I have fished with surface flies for largemouth and smallmouth bass in ponds, lakes, reservoirs, canals, and quarry pits in the South and as far north as Ontario. Bass are also caught on underwater flies and found in moving water, but my preference is for still water and the chance of bringing them to the surface. Over the years, I've cast from various boat "platforms," ranging from wooden rowboats to the current custom-designed bass boats that are made of fiberglass. These are carpeted and boast elevated bucket seats and an electric trolling motor pedal that sits right under your foot.

Although it is easy to get used to motorized "rowing," it is my unfulfilled dream to have my own leaky wooden rowboat on a lake somewhere nearby, into which I can jump on a summer's evening to spend a couple of hours lazing along in pursuit of bass.

Wooden—and leaky—will give me the nice, slow speed I want in covering water. One pull on the oars and I'll be able to make three or four presentations to likely bass cover without any feeling of "hurry up, before you've passed this place" as I would experience in a boat with an electric motor. I want it like it used to be.

The aura of bass fishing is one of complete relaxation with a hint of excitement to come. Bass are unpredictable, aggressive, and scrappy. Some anglers believe that inch for inch and pound for pound, bass are the gamest fish that swim. Smallmouths are more likely to fit that description than are largemouths, but for me it is the anticipation of the strike, of either species, on a surface bass bug that holds the most intrigue.

Bass burst through the water's surface so explosively that a natural bait would surely die of a heart attack. I prefer not to see them coming to the fly, so that it is a complete surprise, compounded by the antici- pation built up beforehand. Let me tell you what it's like.

A summer evening. A quiet lake; no dwellings. Lily pads and sunken logs, frogs croaking to each other, blackbirds flitting among the cattails before it gets dark. A mosquito hums and goes by. The moon starts up over the nearby hill. The creek of the oars and the sounds of the fly line and bass bug swishing through the air are all you can hear as the frogs suddenly fall silent. The deer-hair bug lands with a *plop* in an opening in the lily pads. Silence descends again as I wait for all of the ripples to disappear from the surface—like Dad used to do it. It seemed so long to wait, back then. But not now. I'm anticipating. It's time for one twitch of the bug. The fly line is under my rod hand and when I have drawn all the slack out of it, I give it a sudden pull through the water and *pow*! a largemouth erupts from the water to take the fly. It keeps climbing upward with the fly still not set in its mouth and then lands with a loud *splat*. I strike to set the hook, but it is too late, the fly is mine again. I missed.

Now I am again aware of the frogs. The rowboat moves slowly along the shore and the glow of the low-hung moon adds mystery to the surroundings. The lily pads end temporarily and a half-sunken log is the next likely cover to explore. My first cast goes between the pads and the log. This time, after waiting for the ripples to disappear, I move the bug rather rapidly back toward the boat, using the line strip method with the rod tip low to chug it. I'm full of anticipation again. There is no action, but perhaps the disturbance woke some- body up!

My next cast goes to the same place and my tactics are the same until I get near the log, and then I dead-stop the bug. And twitch it. Anticipation. Another twitch. Nothing; just anticipation. I twitch it and stop it all the way back to the boat. No bass seems to care.

The thumb hold, with your thumb on the inside of the bass's lower jaw, keeps him quiet while you remove the fly with your other hand.

A tiny pull on the oars lets me put the next cast on the far side of the log and go back to my first tactic, waiting for the ripples to disappear before I make the rapid chugging retrieve. But I never get the chance to retrieve it, and this time I am *not* anticipating the explosion as the dark and deep-bodied outline of a hungry largemouth bass engulfs my fly. As he turns downward, I set the hook and he dives, only to come up a few seconds later in a beautiful moonlit leap, shaking his head from side to side as he tries to get rid of the fly. I move the rod in unison with his moves, creating a little tension so he won't get purchase on the bulky bug.

As he falls back into the water, I take the advantage and put pressure on him to keep him from wrapping the line or leader around the log. I move him toward the boat, but he suddenly surges under it, taking line. I let him go, leaning over the side and stabbing the water with my rod for half its length to keep in touch. I work my rod around the boat and come up on the other side, the open-water side, waiting again for the least sign of his slowing down. He jumps and then jumps again. I take the advantage once more as he crashes back into the water. With a low sideward angle on the rod I pressure him toward where I sit and then raise the rod to slide him next to the boat, taking him by surprise.

Quickly, I reach down and grip him by his lower jaw with my thumb in his mouth, his large mouth I might add, and lift him from the water to admire. He remains quiet (the grip has this effect) while I back out the fly. I thank him for giving me the chance to see him in action, and I think about the next angler who'll have the same thrill as I head him back toward his log cover, none the worse for wear.

Heading back to the boat landing, I wear a big smile on my face that reaches through my whole body.

For the fishing described above you will be sitting down and casting a bulky fly, one cast after another, until a bass interrupts the routine. It can be tiring unless you have someone with whom to share the time. The tackle that most men use, a 9-foot rod for a #9 line, is likely to be too heavy unless you've trained for it, but a 9-foot rod is necessary, because of your sitting position, to lift the bulky flies well up over your head.

Start with a 9-foot rod for a 7-weight line, in as few ounces of rod weight as will do the job. A floating, weight-forward line and a short 4- to 6-foot leader ending at 10-pound-test will complete the outfit.

Do include weedless underwater flies in your equipment. You may be blanked on the surface, and bass love cover that may render your regular hooks ineffective.

On the subject of casting, bass flies can be difficult to get off the water cleanly on the backcast—unless you know the trick. Lift the fly line first, right to the bug, then snap the bug off. For the rest of the backcast, wait until line, leader, and fly are completely straightened behind you before starting forward.

Largemouth and smallmouth bass are sometimes found in the same waters. Generally we think of smallmouths as northern bass because they like lower water temperatures and largemouths as everyman's bass because they prefer warmer water and inhabit every one of the lower forty-eight states. The largemouth world record is 22 pounds plus and was taken in Georgia; the smallmouth record is 10 pounds plus and was taken in Kentucky. (Smallmouths are being bred that can stand warmer water.) A 4-pound smallmouth and a 6- to 10-pound largemouth are big bass for us ordinary folks.

There are two ways to tell the difference between the two bass without having to count scale rows. First, a vertical line through the center of the eye will pass behind the "small mouth" but touches the edge on the large mouth. The second indicator is that, in profile, the smallmouth's forehead is rounded while the largemouth's forehead has a dent in it.

Just like other fish species, the biggest bass hang out in deep water and eat minnows. If you like surface fishing as I do, though, you live for the day when one of the full-grown mamas will come busting through the surface after your offering. As I said, it's the anticipation.

Panfish and Pickerel

Bass are the stars of warm-water fishing, but don't pass up a chance to fly fish for panfish or pickerel. "Panfish" is a group that includes bluegills, perch, calico bass, crappies, and so on. The mouths of bluegills are relatively tiny and I love to hear the smack sound when they take surface flies. Panfish can be delightful eating and perch filets were a specialty at our house when my younger son, Stuart, at the age of five, was an expert at catching them from our pond. Introducing a

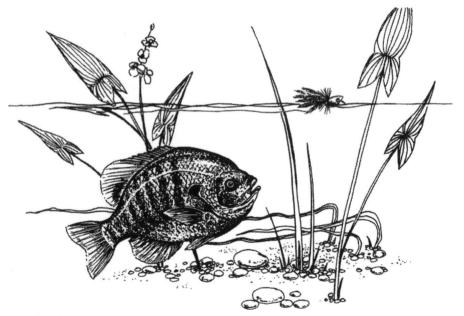

Bluegill

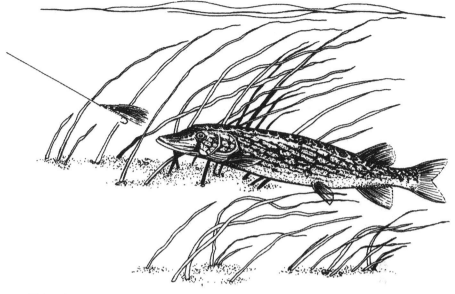

Pickerel

youngster to fly fishing by way of panfish is the best starting point I can think of.

Although bass take flies at both slow and fast speeds of retrieve, the panfish group tends to be less aggressive, so both slow and stop action may be more effective. Use tackle that will make these small species fun to catch: a short, light, 7- or 7½-foot fly rod for a #4 line or, of course, your all-purpose trout rod.

Pickerel are in the aggressive category. They will hide out in grass or behind obstacles. Catlike, they wait to pounce on baitfish, which are their primary food, so you'll need streamers to get their attention. The toothy pickerel's strike is ferocious, the high point of the catch, after which they may surrender and come in like logs.

Northern pike are a big cousin of the pickerel and in eastern Canada they often inhabit the grassy areas of the same lakes as do smallmouth bass. A 7-weight outfit cast with careful timing can handle the large streamer flies for the short to medium casting distances necessary. Pike's teeth are infamous so use a short, stout leader and attach a 4- to 6-inch wire leader between it and the fly.

Pike up to 25 pounds have been taken on a fly in Labrador but, generally, North America's large pike are in the Northwest Territories in such super-sized lakes as Great Slave and Great Bear. Europe has even larger pike, especially in Sweden; a September fishery has been developed there for fly anglers.

In Great Britain in the fifteenth century, Dame Juliana knew the pike well: *"The pike is a good fish, but because he devours so many of his own kind as well as of others, I love him the less."*

17

Saltwater Flats Fishing: Bonefish, Permit, and Tarpon

Wading a stream for trout, Atlantic salmon, or steelhead is the ultimate *individual* challenge in our sport. A different kind of fishing that can be just as exciting centers in the saltwater "flats" of tropical areas. The hot spots are the subtropical Florida Keys, Central America, and the Caribbean, and, for bonefish, at least one area of the Pacific: Christmas Island, fifteen hundred miles south of Hawaii.

The saltwater flats are open, shallow-water areas onto which bonefish, tarpon, and permit cruise with the tide to look for crustaceans and mollusks in the sediment and growth covering the coral bottom.

Fishing for these species as well as for others such as barracuda, redfish, and sea trout is a combination of hunting and fishing. In stream fishing you fish the moving water; on the flats you fish the moving fish. The hunting part is finding the fish and, with luck, seeing them before they see you. Then a perfect presentation must be made, with as few strokes of the rod as possible, to intercept the fish with your fly. Quickness is the key, and, if you are successful, the fun really begins after the strike.

Bonefish and permit will *streak* across the flats to make sizzling runs of a hundred yards or more, and tarpon offer a different thrill because of their size and magnificent leaps. With all three you'll be challenged to reel your fly line back in for minutes at a time. (To avoid the ache that will reach back to the shoulder blade of your reeling arm, a pretrip training program using an egg beater can build your endurance.)

I love being on the flats. No matter how much stress was involved in leaving unfinished matters at home or in the hassle of winter travel to a warmer climate, within fifteen minutes of settling into the fishing I am mentally relaxed. All cares fall away and problems, suddenly seen and analyzed from a different perspective, are solved or put on hold. Perhaps it's the flats' built-in atmosphere of clarity. You can see right to the bottom of the water around you and through the clean air to the horizon.

Beneath the open sky, the overall color effect of your surroundings can range from creamy white to pale yellow and, as your skiff travels from flat to flat, the sun can produce a kaleidescope of blues and greens, often contrasted, surprisingly, with browns and blacks. Incredible beauty!

As the guide poles you quietly over the shallow areas and both sets of eyes search for fish, you'll find yourself in a mood of relaxed concentration. The sounds of birds may disturb the silence as they chatter and call in and around the mangrove islands. Gulls, terns, pelicans, flamingos, and roseate spoonbills inhabit the flats; sandpipers and many other small wading birds are also common. Herons may lift out of the mangroves to startle you, after your intrusion has startled them. Occasionally you may spot an osprey's nest in a tall, dead tree and, in time, its inhabitants. You'll like the flats.

Bonefish, the Gray Ghosts

Beautiful they are not, particularly when compared to most other fish caught on a fly. Bonefish are bottom feeders and so their mouths are on the underside of their heads, much like freshwater suckers. Out of the water their color is almost pure silver, textured with longitudinal lines and contrasted with a smooth white belly. In the water they take on subtle colorings from their surroundings. After they have made their sizzling runs they tend to circle the boat, if played with fairly light pressure, and at this time their reflection of the background makes them appear beautifully iridescent. In size, bonefish range from 1½ to 15 pounds.

The toughest part of this fishing is to *see* the fish so that you can make the cast accurately. To meet that challenge you must become

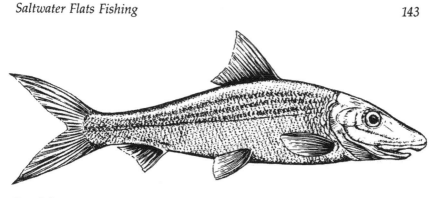

Bonefish

familiar with the flat's bottom to learn its character. Then anything that isn't the bottom may be a bonefish! And what a varied bottom it can be. Ideally it is absolutely clear and light colored, but it can be mottled with grassy clumps or debris from mangrove-island growth. Bits and pieces of debris can look like oncoming bonefish and give the illusion of movement if you forget that the boat is gliding silently forward. Surface waves make shadows that sweep across the bottom to add to the intrigue. It's challenging!

First-timers may take a while to develop their skill at seeing fish. You can't daydream and just stare at the water; your eyes must penetrate it. Bonefish sometimes appear to be gray, sometimes dark (when the sun is obscured); often it is only their black shadows that give them away. You'll want to visually "sweep" the water, from side to side and forward and back at the same time, to keep up with the guide's search. Occasionally look far ahead, out of casting range, for moving shadows, wakes, or "nervous" water, as it is called, from oncoming fish. Otherwise, keep the search within casting range.

Bonefish may appear singly or in schools as they cruise the flats. When your shrimp imitation lands in their path a few feet ahead of the lead fish, let it sink to the bottom, then make short strips of six inches or so to make the fly "hop" through the water, lifting up and settling down much like a grasshopper does on land. The take of a bonefish is usually soft, so it is a good idea to watch both the fly and the fish carefully to see the hookup.

When bonefish are feeding, they dig their noses into the soft sand above the coral bottom and, if the water is shallow, their tails waving above the surface will catch the sunlight and give away their position. Now you must cast the fly to get their attention without spooking them. Put it a foot or two in front of one of them. Let it sink, then hop it enticingly.

Nose "tracks," which are shaped like the forward section of your shoe sole, are one of the visible signs that say "bonefish have fed here." Permit leave tracks too, in a slightly larger version.

Your guide will see 99 percent of the available fish before you do and tell you where to cast, whether or not you see the fish. He'll use a clock for reference (the center of the bow is 12 o'clock) saying, "Bonefish, ten o'clock, thirty feet." If he doesn't give you all of that information, call it to his attention. Under the pressure of time, everything matters, so the best idea is to discuss this part of the fishing in the first few minutes of the first day. Make a few trial presentations to be sure you both agree on judgment of distances.

The word "discussion" is a bit far-fetched in the Caribbean because most bonefish guides speak their native Spanish and know only limited English. Many bonefish camps provide guests with a flats-fishing "dictionary," a glossary of fishing terms such as *strip, fast, slow, stop, gone,* in both Spanish and English.

Another word you'll hear from the guide is "spooked!" as the bonefish takes off, frightened by the nearness of the boat or a cast that wasn't perfect. Although you have probably been told how little room for error there is in bonefishing, there are times that break the rules. More than once I've had a single fish suddenly appear at a distance I knew was too close to the boat. Instead of spooking, though, it allowed me to present the fly and then took it like a child who was waiting for dessert.

You'll experience a high when you occasionally spot fish before the guide does, and you'll be better at spotting on the second day than on the first. If you do this kind of fishing just once a year, though, you'll probably have to learn to see all over again on the first day or two of each trip. Don't feel badly about it; it happens to everyone and the guides understand that.

As you search for bonefish you'll see stingrays, leopard rays, barracuda, and an occasional shark, among other things. The rays often don't see the boat until it is on top of them and then they take off in a cloud of mud that will startle you out of a reverie.

Barracuda are wonderful sport on any tackle but especially on the fly rod. With bonefish as your primary quarry, you'll need to take along a backup fly rod with a wire leader section ahead of the fly to use when a barracuda appears. These fierce and toothy predators are attracted to flies that resemble needlefish, another inhabitant of the flats. They will "greyhound" upon feeling the hook, taking one jump after another with greater speed (in my experience) than almost any other fish. If the change from bonefish rod to barracuda rod will take

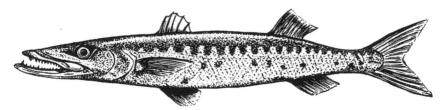

Barracuda

too long, a lightweight spinning rod with 4- to 6-pound-test line can give you this bonus action.

Leaving the boat to wade the flats gives you that independent and involved feeling, even with barracuda for companions. (If you move toward a barracuda, he'll retreat, but he might eat your hooked bonefish.) Because of the occasional incidence of spiny creatures you'll need to wear wading shoes to protect your feet. There is a special flats version made of neoprene with hard soles, or you can use your standby boat shoes.

Thinking about wading immediately brings back an experience I had in Ascension Bay on Mexico's Yucatan Peninsula. Lee and the guide had gone off together and had left me to fish alone, at my request. The day was hot, dead calm, and completely overcast. It was eerie. I couldn't tell where the water stopped and the sky began; there was no horizon. With no mangrove islands anywhere near me for reference, I felt as if I were at the center of the universe, the smallest possible dot on the face of the earth.

As I stood still, searching the water, a bonefish moved into my vision, startlingly black against the clear bottom. I was holding several loops of line and easily made a cast of forty-five feet that I thought would reach him. It fell well short of the fish. I retrieved the line and cast all of the loops. Short once more! I took more line off the reel. In the dead calm air I worked to put as much force into the cast as possible. Still, I couldn't reach a fish that looked to be within my range. I pulled in my line and checked the distance marks on it. I was casting fifty feet of fly line, plus the length of the rod and the length of the leader, for a total of sixty-seven feet! It was my depth perception that was out of whack in those climatic conditions.

As I moved in to close the gap between us, the bonefish did his ghost act and disappeared.

The Elusive Permit

Permit, which range up to 30 pounds or more in size, are found in the same general areas as are bonefish but in slightly deeper water. They too feed on crabs, shrimp, and other crustaceans. Flat-sided, deep-bodied fish, they have a distinctive scythelike dorsal fin that, along with the tail, is dark enough to look black. They appear dark on top and white or silvery in the bulk of the body, although they often reflect the color of their surroundings.

This species is perfect for an angler in her third stage of development—that of catching the most difficult fish. If bonefish can be characterized as the foot soldiers of the flats, then permit are the cavalry. The fishing method is the same except that the flies are slightly larger and crab imitations are the primary pattern. Permit are bigger and faster than bonefish, so lengthen the strip on the retrieve to a foot or more. Your guide will coach you.

Permit

When a school of permit can be observed unalarmed, they move through the water like a flock of birds weaves through the sky, leaning gracefully on the curves, changing their direction in an instant, appearing to be fully enjoying what they are doing. Majestic, commanding, filled with an incredible energy that is transmitted from fish to angler like an electrical charge, the permit remains elusive for the fly-rod angler. Although they are easy to catch on live crabs (just as brook trout can always be caught on worms), after presenting flies to a dozen schools and many individual fish, and after comparing notes with other anglers, it would seem that nothing that matters to us matters to the permit: the size, color, or action given to the fly. This fish is either eating or not eating! Perhaps the answer lies in better crab imitations.

Because of their shape, permit can be extremely difficult to land if they use their flat sides as leverage against the angler's tackle. But oh, what excitement! I've caught two small ones that weighed between 6 and 8 pounds, as of this writing, but most memorable are the larger ones that followed but didn't take my fly. Fishing for these creatures is extraordinary fishing! You can't help but be moved in their presence.

Tarpon

Because of the tarpon's size relative to the angler and her tackle, these giant members of the herring family, weighing between 40 and 200 pounds, are undisputedly the top challenge of saltwater flats fishing. As in bonefish and permit fishing, you cast only when you see the fish, but tarpon are extremely hard to hook well because of their bony mouths. The hook is set with three or more hard pulls backward. On the average, only one out of seven that are hooked are landed. But once hooked these "silver kings," which may be bigger and heavier than you are, usually jump and jump and *jump* at the beginning of the fight. Once you have fought one for a half hour or more, it is possible that you may feel relief if it throws the hook, having had the best of it with the jumps and, of course, the strike. The strike is the high point for me because it is all so visual: seeing the fish, casting the

Tarpon

fly, fish overtaking the fly, the mouth opening, the mouth closing, the connection!

My introduction to tarpon fishing was in May 1963. My hostess, Lynette Siman, didn't fly fish and so paired me with her husband, Pete, and guide Clarence Lowe. West of Islamorada, in Florida Bay, we staked out on the edge of a channel to watch and wait. We didn't have to wait long. Clarence saw the pod first, about a quarter of a mile away, and told me where to look. They were black dots at that distance, about six in all, and there followed several minutes of watching them getting bigger and bigger and taking shape before they reached us. The tarpon's average length was about 6 feet, which meant that their weight was over 75 pounds. Instead of swimming right on by, they formed a daisy chain right in front of us. (This circular formation is a part of the mating procedure.)

Pete had given me first shot and I was up on the bow with my fly line spread at my feet and my 4/0 streamer fly in hand. Clarence instructed me to cast to the middle of the left side of the circle of fish, which was moving counterclockwise. With a pounding heart and dry throat I did as I was told and started to retrieve the fly in one-and-a-half- to two-foot-long strips. Bingo! One strip and a huge mouth opened and engulfed my red-and-yellow fly. As I set the hook, the connection felt so good I held . . . too long! The huge tarpon moved its head opposite my pressure and broke the 12-pound leader. I was embarrassed when I realized that I had handled the tarpon as if it were a largemouth bass, the biggest fish I had ever hooked previously, thinking I could control it in the same way.

Even though I didn't catch a tarpon in that first experience, I felt lucky to have had a part in a saltwater drama with such huge creatures as the actors. I was thrilled to have hooked a 6-footer on my first cast, brief though the connection was. I think the magic in fly fishing is that it puts you in touch with so many of Mother Nature's creatures that would otherwise be inaccessible to you. Tarpon are in the thrilling "monster" class, and that first experience hooked me.

My friend Kay Brodney, in her own words "a fly-fishin' fool," took a tarpon of 137½ pounds in the late 1960s with Florida guide Stu Apte. Kay's fish was only 10 to 15 pounds under the official record at the time and it was quite a feat with her 10-weight rod. There are a lot more women out there now but they are releasing fish they know won't break the world record. Every June, Islamorada hosts a three-day women's world invitational tarpon fly (release) tournament, but so far the largest fish have averaged only 120 pounds.

Male tarpon fishermen and guides will almost universally tell you that you must use a 12- or 13-weight outfit to catch tarpon. Not so! I was once the subject of an outdoor column by the *Miami Herald*'s Vic Dunaway because I landed an 84-pound tarpon on a 9-weight rod. The outfit was the heaviest outfit I owned and matched my strength. I could use it without excessive fatigue. It hooked and landed the tarpon. It may take a little longer to land a fish on lighter tackle, which may be one of the subtle reasons guides and companions discourage it, but if you can play a fish well, and your guide follows the fish to keep it within reasonable distance so you can put maximum pressure on it, there should be no complaints. I landed my 84-pound fish in twenty-five minutes. Be warned, however, that tarpon, like other fish, are individuals; you can have an easy fish or a devil!

Use the heaviest tackle you can handle well or, conversely, the lightest tackle that will do the job. If the outfit is too heavy, you won't cast accurately and you won't have any staying power during the playing of the fish. Then you'll give up tarpon fishing because it's no fun.

Preparations for Flats Fishing

Presenting a fly to a fish moving through the water is like shooting game birds; you must lead the target to make the interception. The element of time requires an efficiency of motion to present the fly before the fish gets out of range.

The ideal technique is called a "quick cast." It begins with an unhurried cast made to your long cast limit well before you have spotted any fish. The shooting line is then retrieved and spread carefully on the bow platform and, with most of the heavy "head" section out of the rod tip and the leader and fly in your hand, you wait to spot the fish. To make the presentation, you make a roll-cast forward into the air, followed by one backcast on which you shoot line, and finish with a forward cast to the fish, shooting more line as necessary. That is, ideally. You can always make more than one backcast if you have the time, but another factor with these fish is that they can be spooked by excessive false casting at close range.

Tackle for bonefish and permit can be in the 6- or 7-weight category, backed up by an #8/9. Use a #9 or #10, as I do, for tarpon. Training is a must, for light or heavy tackle, to master the quick cast and to build muscles for reeling and holding pressure on big fish. If you use trout tackle for bonefish, the outfit will weigh roughly half a pound. Tarpon tackle will probably weigh a full pound, even in a "light" outfit. Newton said it best: "The heavier the object, the more force required to set it into motion or bring it to a stop."

Your training program should include the following exercises:

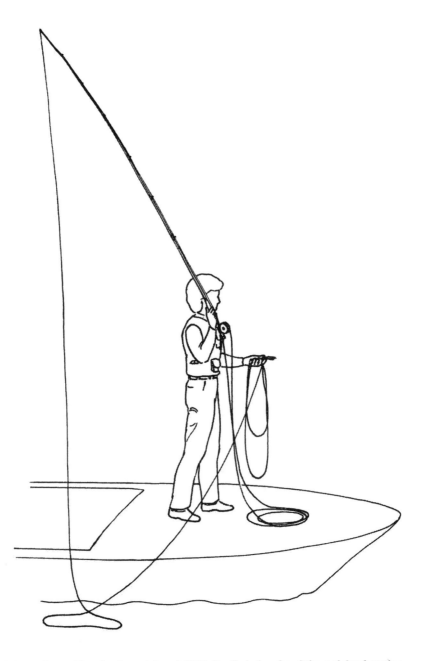

The ready position for the quick cast. With the fly in hand and the weighted section of the fly line out of the rod tip, you can make a presentation with only one backcast.

1. Practice casting outdoors with the whole outfit and develop your ability to shoot line on the backcast for the quick-cast technique.

2. With tarpon tackle, tie your 12- or 15-pound-test leader tippet to something stationary and hold playing pressure on it in increments of minutes, increasing the time gradually.

3. Indoors, use the butt of the rod with the reel attached to build casting strength. Make back and forward strokes to simulate the quick-cast sequence. Remember that each stroke is an acceleration to a stop and the stop is what requires the hand strength.

4. Practice reeling with an egg beater or with a reel on the rod butt to build up arm and shoulder muscles. Count the turns of the handle and build the number until you can do five hundred at a time.

Clothing and Accessories

Heat, cold, wind, sun, and rain are with you wherever and whenever you go fishing. The layers just change thickness. Use khaki, pastels, and white to blend with the background.

In intense heat, wear 100 percent cotton or the newer synthetics found in "tarpon wear" lines, such as that which Simms has initiated, with Coolmax mesh vents behind the armpits. These vented synthetics compare favorably with cotton and are easily washed out in camp. A member of our bonefishing group washed his by wearing it in the shower and soaping it up, on himself. It was "clean" and dry by morning.

Orvis sells nice cargo-type pants with zip-off legs that solve the heat and sun-exposure problems. Other mail-order catalogs offer similar pants. Winter bonefishing in Florida, the Bahamas, and the Yucatan Peninsula can be subject to the cold fronts that affect the continental United States, and temperatures may fall to 50 degrees or below. Even when it is warm, you can be chilly in fast-running, open flats boats between fishing areas. Take a windbreaker with a concealed hood and a cotton sweater, or one of the new synthetic, toasty-warm jackets to wear under it. Long underwear can make sleeping more comfortable in 40-degree tropical nights.

Sunscreen, rated more than 20, should be put on more often than the directions indicate to avoid producing a "raccoon face." Remember, too, that you can get sunburned through lightweight shirts.

Finding the right headgear for flats fishing takes some research. Hats have always been a problem for me; I just don't look good in them and feel hot and encumbered when wearing one. Walking through Bloomingdale's one day I noticed a beautiful hot-pink hat with a three-inch-wide, floppy brim and an attached scarf, all in cool cotton. I thought it looked rather striking and pictured myself at last being able to wear a designer hat on a bonefish flat just like the ads in *Vogue* would have me do. Feminine it was, but, unfortunately, the floppy brim had a mind of its own and there was always a dip in the way as I searched the water for fish. I had to move my head mechanically to scan the water and to make up for my loss of peripheral vision. When a gust of wind touched me, the whole brim went up and down in waves. It was a hilarious and short-lived indulgence with a sit-on-the-beach hat. Now it sits in my closet awaiting a day that will probably never come.

I've settled for visors, like those made for tennis and golf. With the open crown, these work well for winter fishing when the sun isn't too hot and there is a breeze. Otherwise it's back to the popular fisherman's hat with bill and flaps—but in the new pastel colors.

Sudden showers in the tropics are usually intense and can really beat you down. The windbreaker you carry can be a dual purpose rain jacket, but it won't keep your bottom dry if the shower lasts awhile. Your choices are a short raincoat with hood, a poncho, a two-piece rain suit, or a one-piece, full-length raincoat of the type used by northern boat fishermen.

Last, but not least, no matter where you are going don't forget your Polaroids!

Camps

When you leave the United States for saltwater flats fishing, you are likely to be in remote areas. Almost all camps are comfortable and provide many amenities, but there will be little inconveniences such as generators turned off overnight or during the day when clients are out fishing. Some will ask you not to use a hair dryer, saying "the natural look is in."

The tropics breed bugs, including palmetto bugs (related to northern cockroaches), spiders, and scorpions. Scorpions are not deadly but they will give you a nasty sting. Check wet and dark places such as your wading shoes before inserting feet. Take clear zippered bags for your underwear and keep your gear bags zipped up in your room.

Carefully shake out your clothing and shoes before putting them on.

Take a flashlight, face cloths and, of course, medication for Montezuma's revenge. Pepto-Bismol is getting high marks for help in this respect. One friend suggests taking it for three days before going to a tropical area and then using more only if, and when, you need it.

On Being in an Open Boat All Day

In the 1960s I was lucky enough to fish in the Islamorada Gold Cup tarpon tournament as part of my job for the Garcia Corporation. The tournament rules allowed a choice of fly, plug, or spinning tackle and my friend, Lynette Siman, competed with spinning tackle. At the end of the long, hot fishing days in May, which began at 6:15 A.M. and ended at the dock at 4:00 P.M., I would take off my fishing hat, wash away the sun lotion (which had by then become a paste), and look as though I'd been put through a clothes wringer. Lynette, who had been out as long as I had, would look as if she had just done her hair! As her house guest, I discovered that she put her crown up in rollers before she put on her fishing hat and, later in the day, a few minutes in the ladies room at the marina brought her coif back up to par.

Memories of those long days in a boat bring to mind something every woman has to think about. What happens when nature calls? I honestly think that our numbers in this particular field of fishing may be unusually low because of this kind of problem. To solve it, don't be embarrassed; be practical. Your options read something like this:

1. Go ashore on a mangrove island and take your chances with the sand flies.

2. Ask your guide to turn his head and sit over the edge of the gunwale.

3. Ask your guide to run the motor in neutral and go in a bucket. (The sound of the motor gives you a little privacy.)

4. Cover yourself with a poncho on the gunwale or on the bucket.

5. Or, do as I do. I have trained myself not to urinate for that nine-hour period.

I have one cup of tea for breakfast and visit the ladies' room just before the boat leaves the dock. I drink one carbonated beverage with lunch or sip it over a period of time and use little fruit-drop candies to relieve a dry mouth. I ask the guide not to bounce me too hard on the return trip and, if I keep my mind off the subject, I can walk slowly to the ladies' room when I leave the boat.

This may or may not be healthy, but no liquid means no pressure. I make up for not drinking during the fishing day by drinking more liquids than usual in the remaining hours of the day and night. I cannot last nine hours when I am cold or it is raining. It is a matter of knowing your body chemistry and making practical decisions.

There is another discomfort peculiar to women in this kind of fishing, and that is bosom bouncing as the boat is run at top speed. The guide runs the boat from the most comfortable position, which is even with or just ahead of the motor. Every place forward in the boat gets the brunt of the pounding. Any angler can really get bounced and jarred, to the point of having a headache, but when your bosom starts to bounce, you can only fold your arms over your chest and/or ask the guide to slow down a bit. I can hear the guides giggling over that one.

Stand up for yourself. Anytime the way the boat is run causes you extreme discomfort, ask that it be changed. You might kiddingly tell the guide that if he wants to be tipped he must make you more comfortable. You can decide later if you were kidding. You have nothing to lose.

18

Blue-water Fly Rodding

T he fly fisherman's world now extends to the oceans, not only for dinner-table fish such as bluefish, mackerel, and striped bass, but also to sailfish and marlin for top-of-the-line sport and challenge. The adventure of blue-water fly rodding is relatively new, only twenty-five to thirty years old, but is growing by leaps and bounds in popularity.

Finding the fish, the search, begins early in the day at Golfito Camp in southwestern Costa Rica. Lee and I leave the dock at 6:30 A.M. in a 23-foot Mako for the two-hour run to the fishing grounds. For someone who suffers from mal de mer, the Pacific is much easier to take than the Atlantic, and I enjoy the gentle swells while keeping my eyes on the glassy surface, hoping that something, perhaps a porpoise, will break through to entertain us on the way out. It is January and the temperature is climbing to the eighties. The overhead canopy will give a welcome respite from the hot sun as the day wears on.

At 8:40, Captain Chi Chi puts out two standard trolling rigs to trail poppers of fluorescent red, yellow, and blue with Hawaiian-like "skirts" and we settle down to trolling speed. Our eyes fasten on these hookless teasers.

Ten minutes later a pencillike bill breaks the slick surface behind the left teaser and all three of us utter the word "sail" as we jump into action. Lee starts to reel in the neglected right-side teaser while Chi Chi takes the hot one and brings it in slowly and enticingly to keep the sail interested. I, as the fly rodder, flip the streamer-popper into the water, then pick it up and make a false cast or two (the 9-foot rod takes it well above this small boat's canopy) to extend line. When I drop it, Chi Chi, having put the engine in neutral, literally snatches the teaser out of the water. The frustrated fish looks around for that wonderfully tempting morsel, sees my fly next to his bill and engulfs it.

The sequence in nature is for the sailfish to whack its baitfish prey with its bill to stun it. Helpless, the bait may drift several yards until it is picked up and swallowed. To simulate this with trolling tackle and real bait, the big-game angler must see the strike, then release line to spool out so that the bait drifts freely. (It is just like drifting a dry fly without drag in trout fishing.)

The fly angler is not trolling. After the cast, he imparts action to the fly with stripping motions, and the hook is set when the billfish takes it. If the fish takes the fly broadside, the hooking is easier than if he takes it from behind. Sometimes the sequence occurs in slow motion and other times it's incredibly quick. You may have to see a billfish at your fly more than once to know exactly what is going on. And the fishing gods are fickle: Whether the sailfish takes it, whether the hook is set well, and what happens next will always make an exciting story.

Sailfish are a reasonable challenge for a fly-rod angler because they expend lots of energy jumping, either vertically or in grey-hounding leaps. Tarpon on the flats expend their energy by jumping, too, but they are in shallow water. With a whole ocean in which to try to escape, it is when a billfish goes down, and goes down deep, that you really feel helpless. You can only maintain contact and wait.

A 10- to 12-weight outfit is suitable for this fishing, with at least 250 yards of 30-pound-test Dacron backing behind the fly line. The casting is minimal so you can choose the rod for its playing capabilities. In the newest generation of graphite, my #12 rod weighs 5⅞ ounces. It is also built with a second cork grip above the first, so that when the rod butt is braced against the abdomen or set in a belt socket, the rod hand can move up to get better leverage.

When the fish runs, I let him go, drag free, palming the rim-control reel when possible. There's no way he can be stopped. The danger is in trying. As he takes out line, everything trailing behind

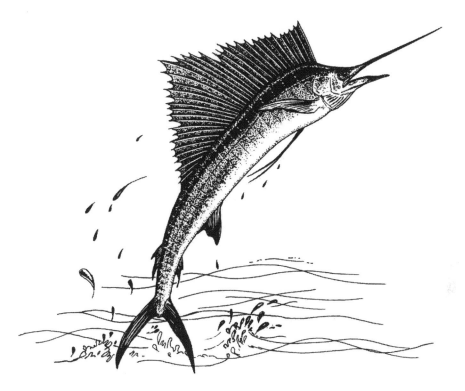

Sailfish

him—which includes the skinny Dacron backing line—creates its own resistance through the water. When a mechanical drag or your hand's palming strengthens that resistance, there is a limit as to what it will take before the weakest part of the tackle, the class tippet (mine is 16-pound-test) breaks. The farther the fish runs, the less drag you want to apply.

Preparation for this kind of fishing consists of training your muscles in reeling and in holding a strain on the leader, just as you would do for tarpon fishing. Using an egg beater for the simulation of reeling and tying your 12- to 16-pound-test tippet to a fence post or other stationary object can give you staying power and confidence in fighting such a fish.

Now my sailfish is heading right for me as I stand at the boat's stern, the rod butt in my belt socket. I reel as fast as I can, but I can't catch up, and when the popper fly shows up on the surface fifty feet away there is no sailfish with it. I lower the rod in sadness and turn to

Lee for sympathy but, as I do, incredibly, the same fish (or is it?) breaks the surface and again picks up the fly. His run is straight away from the stern as I struggle to gain control, hoping that, this time, he has hooked himself well. Straight up out of the water he jumps, fifty yards astern, and his nearly 10-foot length hangs in the air so that we can all get a good look at him. Chi Chi guesses him to be 100 pounds or better, and I feel his full weight as he crashes back into the water.

Thrilling as it is to be attached to a "monster of the deep," I wonder if I'll be able to stand up to the fight for what will surely be an hour or more on this, my first experience. I tell myself to calm down and not race my engine, or I will tire that much more quickly. I start reviewing lessons I've learned from Lee's experience.

Now the fish has disappeared, and I know that he can be anywhere. The density of the water is like the dense brush of land. If your dog goes into it with a trailing rope, the rope shows you where he's been, not where he is. I continue to reel in as fast as I can, pointing the rod to where the line goes into the water. The shoulder blade on my reeling arm begins to ache, because, in spite of what I know about the need to practice reeling, I haven't done it.

Before a blue-water fly-fishing trip, practice holding a strain on a stationary object. This will help minimize playing time.

Chi Chi calls out *"Aquí, Aquí!"* (There! There!) and the fish has leaped once more, behind me this time, 180 degrees from where my fly line enters the water. I haven't picked up enough line to feel his weight as he falls back into the water but I keep reeling and reeling, and aching, never catching up before he spits out the fly, this time for good.

What a lonely feeling it is to be disconnected from a supercharged creature of the ocean! But what a wonderful feeling it was to have been in contact with a Pacific sailfish weighing more than 100 pounds, on a 6-ounce fly rod, for how long? Only *six* minutes!

[*Editor's note:* On March 5, 1991, Joan landed and released a 40-kilo (88-pound) Pacific sailfish off Quepos, Costa Rica. She was aboard Tom Bradwell's *Marlin Azul II* with Captain Joses Enrique. From strike to capture was a brief ten to fifteen minutes.]

My husband, Lee, first heard this as a youngster but doesn't know its origin. I have changed the sex of the angler.

> *When the wind is from the North, the fishergirl should not go forth.*
> *When the wind is from the East, then the fish will bite the least.*
> *When the wind is from the South, it blows the bait in the fish's mouth.*
> *But when the wind is from the West, then the fish will bite the best.*

Appendix

Treatise of Fishing with an Angle

Solomon in his Proverbs says that a good spirit makes a flowering age, that is, a fair age and a long one. And since it is so, I ask this question, "What are the means and the causes that lead a man into a merry spirit?" Truly, in my best judgment, it seems that they are good sports and honest games in which a man takes pleasure without any repentance afterward. Thence it follows that good recreations and honorable pastimes are the cause of a man's fair old age and long life. And therefore, I will now choose among four good sports and honorable pastimes—to wit, among hunting, hawking, fishing, and fowling. The best, in my simple judgment, is fishing, called angling, with a rod and a line and a hook. And thereof I will treat as my simple mind will permit, both for the above-mentioned saying of Solomon and also for the statement that medical science makes in this manner:

Si tibi deficiant medici, medici tibi fiant
Haec tria—mens laeta, labor, et moderatadiaeta.

You shall understand, that is to say, that if a man lacks physician or doctor, he shall make three things his physician and doctor, and he will never need any more. The first of them is a merry thought. The second is work which is not excessive. The third is a moderate diet. First, if a man wishes to be always in merry thoughts and have a glad spirit, he must avoid all quarrelsome company and all places of dispute, where he might have any causes of melancholy. And if he wishes to have a labor which is not excessive, he must then arrange for himself, for his heart's ease and pleasure—without care, anxiety, or trouble—a merry occupation which may rejoice his heart and in which his spirits may have a merry delight. And if he wishes to have a moderate diet, he must avoid all places of debauchery, which is the cause of overindulgence and sickness. And he must withdraw himself to places of sweet and hunger-producing air, and eat nourishing foods and also digestible ones.

Now then I will describe the said sports or games to find out, as truly as I can, which is the best of them; albeit the right noble and very worthy prince, the Duke of York, lately called the Master of Game, has described the joys of hunting, just as I think to describe it and all the others. For hunting, to my mind, is too laborious. For the hunter must always run and follow his hounds, laboring and sweating very painfully. He blows on his horn till his lips blister; and when he thinks he is chasing a hare, very often it is a hedgehog. Thus he hunts and knows not what. He comes home in the evening rain-beaten, scratched, his clothes torn, wet-shod, all muddy, this hound lost and that one crippled. Such griefs happen to the hunter—and many others which, for fear of the displeasure of them that love it, I dare not report. Thus, truly, it seems to me that this is not the best recreation or game of the four mentioned.

The sport and pastime of hawking is laborious and troublesome also, as it seems to me. For often the falconer loses his hawks, as the hunter his hounds. Then his pastime and sport is gone. Very often he shouts and whistles till he is terribly thirsty. His hawk takes to a bough and does not choose to pay him any attention. When he would have her fly at the game, then she wants to bathe. With improper feeding she will get the frounce, the ray, the cray, and many other sicknesses that bring them to the upward flight. Thus, by proof, this is not the best sport and game of the four mentioned.

The sport and game of fowling seems to me poorest of all. For in the winter season the fowler has no luck except in the hardest and coldest weather, which is vexatious. For when he would go to his traps, he cannot because of the cold. Many a trap and many a snare he makes, yet he fares badly. In the morning time, in the dew, he is wet-shod up to his tail. Much more of the same I could tell, but dread of displeasure makes me leave off. Thus, it seems to me that hunting and hawking and also fowling are so toilsome and unpleasant that none of them can succeed nor be the true means of bringing a man into a

merry frame of mind, which is the cause of his long life according to the said proverb of Solomon.

Undoubtedly then, it follows that it must needs be the sport of fishing with a hook. (For every other kind of fishing is also toilsome and unpleasant, often making folks very wet and cold, which many times has been seen to be the cause of great sicknesses.) But the angler can have no cold nor discomfort nor anger, unless he be the cause himself. For he can lose at the most only a line or a hook, of which he can have a plentiful supply of his own making, as this simple treatise will teach him. So then his loss is not grievous, and other griefs he cannot have, except that some fish may break away after he has been caught on the hook, or else that he may catch nothing. These are not grievous, for if the angler fails with one, he may not fail with another, if he does as this treatise teaches—unless there are no fish in the water. And yet, at the very least, he has his wholesome and merry walk at his ease, and a sweet breath of the sweet smell of the meadow flowers, that makes him hungry. He hears the melodious harmony of birds. He sees the young swans, herons, ducks, coots, and many other birds with their broods, which seems to me better than all the noise of hounds, the blasts of horns, and the clamor of birds that hunters, falconers, and fowlers can produce. And if the angler catches fish, surely then *there is no man merrier than he is in his spirit. Also whoever wishes to practice the sport of angling, he must rise early, which thing is profitable to a man in this way. That is, to wit: most for the welfare of his soul, for it will cause him to be holy; and for the health of his body, for it will cause him to be well; also for the increase of his goods, for it will make him rich. As the old English proverb says in this manner: "Whoever will rise early shall be holy, healthy, and happy."*

Thus have I proved, according to my purpose, that the sport and game of angling is the true means and cause that brings a man into a merry spirit, which (according to the said proverb of Solomon and the said teaching of medicine) makes a flowering age and a long one. And therefore, to all you that are virtuous, gentle, and freeborn, I write and make this simple treatise which follows, by which you can have the whole art of angling to amuse you as you please, in order that your age may flourish the more and last the longer.

If you want to be crafty in angling, you must first learn to make your tackle, that is, your rod, your lines of different colors. After that, you must know how you should angle, in what place of the water, how deep, and what time of day; for what manner of fish, in what weather; how many impediments there are in the fishing that is called angling; and especially with what baits for each different fish in every month of the year; how you must make your baits-bread, where you will find the baits, and how you will keep them; and for the most difficult thing, how you are to make your hooks of steel and iron, some for the artificial fly and some for the float and the ground-line, as you will afterward hear all these things expressed openly for your knowledge.

And how you should make your rod skillfully, here I will teach you. You must cut, between Michaelmas and Candlemas, a fair staff, a fathom and a half long and as thick as your arm, of hazel, willow, or aspen; and soak it in a hot oven, and set it straight. Then let it cool and dry for a month. Then take and tie it tight with a cockshoot cord, and bind it to a bench or a perfectly square, large timber. Then take a plumber's wire that is smooth and straight and sharp at one end. And heat the sharp end in a charcoal fire till it is white-hot, and then burn the staff through with it, always straight in the pith at both ends, till the holes meet. And after that, burn it in the lower end with a spit for roasting birds, and with other spits, each larger than the last, and always the largest last; so that you make your hole always taper-wax. Then let it lie still and cool for two days. Untie it then and let it dry in a house-roof in the smoke until it is thoroughly dry. In the same season, take a fair rod of green hazel, and soak it even and straight, and let it dry with the staff. And when they are dry, make the rod fit the hole in the staff, into half the length of the staff. And to make the other half of the upper section, take a fair shoot of blackthorn, crabtree, medlar, or juniper, cut in the same season and well soaked and straightened; and bind them together neatly so that the upper section may go exactly all the way into the above-mentioned hole. Then shave your staff down and make a taper-wax. Then ferrule the staff at both ends with long hoops of iron or latten in the neatest manner, with a spike in the lower end fastened with a running device for pulling your upper section in and out. Then set your upper section a handbreadth inside the upper end of your staff in such a way that it may be as big there as in any other place above. Then, with a cord of six hairs, strengthen your upper section at the upper end as far down as the place where it is tied together; and arrange the cord neatly and tie it firmly in the top, with a loop to fasten your fishing line on. And thus you will make yourself a rod so secret that you can walk with it, and no one will know what you are going to do. It will be light and very nimble to fish with at your pleasure. And for your greater convenience, behold here a picture of it as an example:

After you have made your rod thus, you must learn to color your lines of hair in this manner. First, you must take, from the tail of a white horse, the longest and best hair that you can find; and the rounder it is, the better it is. Divide it into six bunches, and you must color every part by itself in a different color, such as, yellow, green, brown, tawny, russet, and dusky colors.

And to make a good green color on your hair, you must do thus. Take a quart of small ale and put it in a little pan, and add to it half a pound of alum, and put your hair in it, and let it boil softly half an hour. Then take out your hair and let it dry. Then take a half-gallon of water and put it in the pan. And put in it two handfuls of a yellow dye, and press it with a tilestone, and let it boil softly half an hour. And when it is yellow on the scum, put in your hair with half a pound of green vitriol, called copperas, beaten to a powder, and let it boil half-a-mile-way. And then set it down and let it cool five or six hours. Then take out the hair and dry it. And it is then the best green there is for the water. And ever the more you add to it of copperas, the better it is. Or else instead of copperas, use verdigris.

Another way, you can make a brighter green, thus. Dye your hair with blue dye until it is a light blue-gray color. And then seethe it in yellow vegetable dye as I have described, except that you must not add to it either copperas or verdigris.

To make your hair yellow, prepare it with alum as I have explained before, and after that with yellow vegetable dye without copperas or verdigris.

Another yellow you shall make thus. Take a half-gallon of small ale, and crush three handfuls of walnut leaves, and put them together. And put in your hair till it is as deep a yellow as you want to have it.

To make russet hair, take a pint and a half of strong lye and half a pound of soot and a little juice of walnut leaves and a quart of alum; and put them all together in a pan and boil them well. And when it is cold, put in your hair till it is as dark as you want it.

To make a brown color, take a pound of soot and a quart of ale, and seethe it with as many walnut leaves as you can. And when they turn black, set it off the fire. And put your hair in it, and let it lie still until it is as brown as you wish to have it.

To make another brown, take strong ale and soot and blend them together, and put therein your hair for two days and two nights, and it will be a right good color.

To make a tawny color, take lime and water, and put them together; and also put your hair therein four or five hours. Then take it out and put it in tanner's ooze for a day, and it will be as fine a tawny color as is required for our purpose.

The sixth part of your hair, you must keep still white for lines for the dubbed hook, to fish for the trout and grayling, and to prepare small lines for the roach and the dace.

When your hair is thus colored, you must know for which waters and for which seasons they will serve. The green color in all clear water from April till September. The yellow color in every clear water from September till November, for it is like the weeds and other kinds of grass which grow in the waters and rivers, when they are broken. The russet color serves for all the winter until the end of April, as well in rivers as in pools or lakes. The brown color serves for that water that is black, sluggish, in rivers or in other waters. The tawny color for those waters that are heathy or marshy.

Now you must make your lines in this way. First, see that you have an instrument like this picture drawn hereafter. Then take your hair and cut off from the small end a large handful or more, for it is neither strong nor yet dependable. Then turn the top to the tail, each in equal amount, and divide it into three strands. Then plait each part at the one end by itself, and at the other end plait all three together. And put this last end in the farther side of your instrument, the end that has but one cleft. And fix the other end tight with the wedge the width of four fingers from the end of your hair. Then twist each strand the same way and pull it hard; and fasten them in the three clefts

equally tight. Then take out that other end and twist it sufficiently in which-
ever direction it is inclined. Then stretch it a little and plait it so that it will
not come undone. And that is good. And to know how to make your instrument, behold, here it is in a picture. And it is to be made of wood, except the
bolt underneath, which must be of iron.

When you have as many of the lengths as you suppose will suffice for the
length of a line, then you must tie them together with a water knot or else a
duchess knot. And when your knot is tied, cut off the unused short ends a
straw's breadth from the knot. Thus you will make your lines fair and fine,
and also very secure for any kind of fish. And because you should know both
the water knot and also the duchess knot, behold them here in picture.
Contrive them in the likeness of the drawing.

[Illustration missing from original]

You must understand that the subtlest and hardest art in making your
tackle is to make your hooks, for the making of which you must have suitable
files, thin and sharp and beaten small; a semi-clamp of iron; a bender; a pair of
long and small tongs; a hard knife, somewhat thick; an anvil; and a little
hammer. And for small fish, you must make your hooks in this manner, of the
smallest square needles of steel that you can find. You must put the square
needle in a red charcoal fire till it is of the same color as the fire is. Then take it
out and let it cool, and you will find it well tempered for filing. Then raise the
barb with your knife and make the point sharp. Then temper it again, for
otherwise it will break in the bending. Then bend it like the bend pictured
hereafter as an example. And you must make greater hooks in the same way
out of larger needles, such as embroiderers' or tailors' or shoemakers' needles,
or spear points; and of shoemakers' awls, especially, the best hooks are made
for great fish. And the hooks should bend at the point when they are tested;
otherwise they are not good. When the hook is bent, beat the hinder end out
broad, and file it smooth to prevent fraying of your line. Then put it in the fire
again, and give it an easy red heat. Then suddenly quench it in water, and it

will be hard and strong. And that you may have knowledge of your instruments, behold them here in picture portrayed.

Hammer   **Pinchers**   **Wedge**   **Wrest**

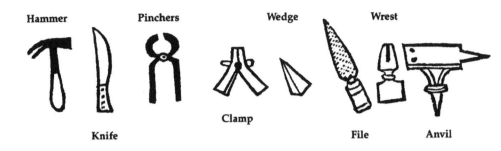

                           Clamp

     Knife   **File**   **Anvil**

When you have made your hooks in this way, then you must set them on your lines, according to size and strength in this manner. You must take fine red silk thread, and if it is for a large hook, then double it, but not twisted. And otherwise, for small hooks, let it be single. And with it, bind the line thick for a straw's breadth from the point where the one end of your hook is to be placed. Then set your hook there, and wrap it with the same thread for two-thirds of the length that is to be wrapped. And when you come to the third part, then turn the end of your line back upon the wrapping, double, and wrap it thus double for the third part. Then put your thread in at the hole twice or thrice, and let it go each time round about the shank of your hook. Then wet the hole and pull it until it is tight. And see that your line always lies inside your hooks and not outside. Then cut off the end of the line and the thread as close as you can, without cutting the knot.

Now that you know with what size hooks you must angle for every fish, I will tell you with how many hairs you must angle for each kind of fish. For the minnow, with a line of one hair. For the growing roach, the bleak, the gudgeon, and the ruff, with a line of two hairs. For the dace and the great roach, with a line of three hairs. For the perch, the flounder, and small bream, with four hairs. For the chevin-chub, the bream, the tench, and the eel, with six hairs. For the trout, grayling, barbel, and the great chevin, with nine hairs. For the great trout, with twelve hairs. For the salmon, with fifteen hairs. And for the pike, with a chalkline made brown with your brown coloring as described above, strengthened with a wire, as you will hear hereafter when I speak of the pike.

Your lines must be weighted with lead sinkers, and you must know that the sinker nearest the hook should be a full foot and more away from it, and every sinker of a size in keeping with the thickness of the line. There are three kinds of sinkers for a running ground-line. And for the float set upon the stationary ground-line, ten weights all joining together. On the running ground-line, nine or ten small ones. The float sinker must be so heavy that the least pluck of any fish can pull it down into the water. And make your sinkers round and smooth so that they do not stick in stones or in weeds. And for the better understanding, behold them here in picture.

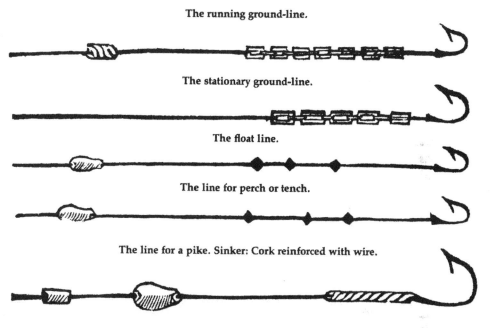

The running ground-line.

The stationary ground-line.

The float line.

The line for perch or tench.

The line for a pike. Sinker: Cork reinforced with wire.

Then you are to make your floats in this manner. Take a good cork that is clean, without many holes; and bore it through with a small hot iron; and put a quill in it, even and straight. Ever the larger the float, the larger the quill and the larger the hole. Then shape it large in the middle and small at both ends, and especially sharp in the lower end, and similar to the pictures following. And make them smooth on a grinding stone, or on a tilestone. And see that the float for one hair is no larger than a pea; for two hairs, like a bean; for twelve hairs, like a walnut; and so every line according to proportion. All kinds of lines that are not for the bottom must have floats, and the running ground-line must have a float. The stationary ground-line without float.

Now I have taught you to make all your tackle. Here I will tell you how you must angle. You shall angle: understand that there are six ways of angling. The one is at the bottom for the trout and other fish. Another is at the bottom at an arch or at a pool, where it ebbs and flows, for bleak, roach, and dace. The *third is with a float for all kinds of fish. The fourth, with a minnow for the trout, without plumb or float. The fifth is running in the same way for roach and dace with one or two hairs and a fly. The sixth is with an artificial fly for the trout and grayling. And for the first and principal point in angling, always keep yourself away from the water, from the sight of the fish, either far*

back on the land or else behind a bush, so that the fish may not see you. For if they do, they will not bite. Also take care that you do not shadow the water any more than you can help, for that is a thing which will soon frighten the fish. And if a fish is frightened, he will not bite for a long time afterward. For all kinds of fish that feed at the bottom, you must angle for them at the bottom, so that your hooks will run or lie on the bottom. And for all other fish that feed above, you must angle for them in the middle of the water, either somewhat beneath or somewhat above. For always the greater the fish, the nearer he will lie to the bottom of the water; and ever the smaller the fish, the more he will swim above. The third good point is: when the fish bites, that you be not too hasty to hook the fish, nor too late. For you must wait till you suppose that the bait is fairly in the mouth of the fish, and then wait no longer. And this is for the ground-line. And for the float, when you see it pulled softly under the water or else carried softly upon the water, then strike. And see that you never strike too hard for the strength of your line, lest you break it. And if you have the fortune to hook a great fish with a small tackle, then you must lead him in the water and labor with him there until he is drowned and overcome. Then take him as well as you can or may, and always beware that you do not hold beyond the strength of your line. And as much as you can, do not let him come out of the end of your line straight from you, but keep him always under the rod and always hold him strait, so that your line can sustain and bear his leaps and his plunges with the help of your crop and of your hand.

Here I will declare to you in what place of the water you must angle. You should angle in a pool or in standing water, in every place where it is at all deep. There is not much choice of such places in a pool. For it is but a prison for fish, and they live for the most part in hunger like prisoners; and therefore it takes the less art to catch them. But in a river, you must angle in every place where it is deep and clear at the bottom, as in gravel or clay without mud or weeds, and especially if there is a kind of whirling of water or a covert—such as a hollow bank or great roots of trees or long weeds floating above in the water—where the fish can cover and hide themselves at certain times when they like. Also it is good to angle in deep, swift streams, and also in waterfalls and weirs, and in floodgates and millraces. And it is good to angle where the water rests by the bank and where the current runs close by and it is deep and clear at the bottom; and in any other places where you can see any fish rise or do any feeding.

Now you must know what time of the day you should angle. From the beginning of May until it is September, the biting time is early in the morning from four o'clock until eight o'clock; and in the afternoon, from four o'clock until eight o'clock, but this is not so good as in the morning. And if there is a cold, whistling wind and it be a dark, lowering day, for a dark day is much better to angle in than a clear day. From the beginning of September until the end of April, angle at any time of the day. Also, many pool fishes will bite best at noontime. And if you see the trout or grayling leap at any time of the day, angle for him with an artificial fly appropriate to that same month. And where the water ebbs and flows, the fish will bite in some place at the ebb, and in some place at the flood. After that, they will rest behind the stakes or pilings and arches of bridges and in other places of that sort.

Here you should know in what weather you must angle: as I said before, in a dark, lowering day when the wind blows softly. And in the summer season when it is burning hot, then it is useless. From September until April in a fair, sunny day, it is right good to angle. And if the wind in that season comes from any part of the east, the weather then is no good. And when there is a great wind, and when it snows, rains, or hails, or there is a great tempest, as with thunder or lightning, or sweltering hot weather, then it is not good for angling.

Now you must know that there are twelve kinds of impediments which cause a man to catch no fish, apart from other common causes that may happen by chance. The first is if your tackle is not adequate or suitably made. The second is if your baits are not good or fine. The third is if you do not angle in biting time. The fourth is if the fish are frightened by the sight of a man. The fifth, if the water is very thick, white or red from any flood recently fallen. The sixth, if the fish do not stir because of the cold. The seventh, if the weather is hot. The eighth, if it rains. The ninth, if it hails or snow falls. The tenth is if there is a tempest. The eleventh is if there is a great wind. The twelfth, if the wind is in the east, and that is worst, for generally, both winter and summer, the fish will not bite then. The west and north winds are good, but the south is best.

And now that I have told you, in all points, how to make your tackle and how you must fish with it, it is reasonable that you should know with what baits you must angle for every kind of fish in each month of the year, which is the gist of the art. And unless these baits are well known by you, all your other skill hitherto avails little to your purpose. For you cannot bring a hook into a fish's mouth without a bait. These baits for every kind of fish and for every month follow here in this manner.

Because the salmon is the most stately fish that any man can angle for in fresh water, therefore I intend to begin with him. The salmon is a noble fish, but he is cumbersome to catch. For generally he is only in deep places of great rivers, and for the most part he keeps to the middle of the water, so that a man cannot come at him. And he is in season from March until Michaelmas, in which season you should angle for him with these baits, when you can get them. First, with an earthworm in the beginning and end of the season. And also with a grubworm that grows in a dunghill. And especially with an excellent bait that grows on a water-dock plant. And he does not bite at the bottom but at the float. Also you may catch him (but this is seldom seen) with an artificial fly at such times as he leaps, in like manner and way as you catch a trout or a grayling. And these baits are well proven baits for the salmon.

The trout, because he is a right dainty fish and also a right fervent biter, we shall speak next of him. He is in season from March until Michaelmas. He is in clean gravel bottom and in a stream. You can angle for him at all times with a lying or running ground-line, except in leaping time and then with an artificial fly; and early with a running ground-line, and later in the day with a float-line. You must angle for him in March with a minnow hung on your hook by the lower nose, without float or sinker, drawing it up and down in the stream till you feel him hooked. In the same time, angle for him with a ground-line with an earthworm as the surest bait. In April, take the same baits, and also the lamprey, otherwise called "seven eyes," also the cankerworm that grows in a great tree, and the red snail. In May, take the stone fly and the grubworm under the cow turd, and the silkworm, and the bait that grows on a fern leaf. In June, take an earthworm and nip off the head, and put a codworm on your hook in front of it. In July, take the big red worm and the codworm together. In August, take a flesh fly and the big red worm and the fat of bacon, and bind them about your hook. In September, take the earthworm and the minnow. In October, take the same, for they are special for the trout at all times of the year. From April to September the trout leaps; then angle for him with an artificial fly appropriate to the month. These flies you will find at the end of this treatise, and the months with them.

The grayling, also known as the umber, is a delicious fish to man's mouth. You can catch him just as you do the trout, and these are his baits. In March and in April, the earthworm. In May, the green worm, a little ringed worm, the dock canker, and the hawthorn worm. In June, the bait that grows between the tree and the bark of an oak. In July, a bait that grows on a fern leaf; and the big red worm, and nip off the head and put a codworm on your hook in front of it. In August, the earthworm, and a dock worm. And all the year afterward, an earthworm.

The barbel is a sweet fish, but it is a queasy food and a perilous one for man's body. For commonly, he introduces the fevers; and if he is eaten raw, he may be the cause of a man's death, as has often been seen. These are his baits. In March and in April, take fair, fresh cheese, lay it on a board, and cut it in small square pieces the length of your hook. Then take a candle and burn it on the end at the point of your hook until it is yellow. And then bind it on your hook with arrowmaker's silk, and make it rough like a welbede. This bait is good for all the summer season. In May and June, take the hawthorn worm and the big red worm; nip off the head and put a codworm on your hook in front; and that is a good bait. In July, take the earthworm chiefly and the hawthorn worm together. Also the water-dock leaf worm and the hornet worm together. In August and for all the year, take mutton fat and soft cheese, of each the same amount, and a little honey; and grind or beat them together a long time, and work it until it is tough. Add to it a little flour, and make it into small pellets. And that is a good bait to angle with at the bottom. And see to it that it sinks in the water, or else it is not good for this purpose.

The carp is a dainty fish, but there are only a few in England, and therefore I will write the less about him. He is a bad fish to catch, for he is so strongly reinforced in the mouth that no weak tackle can hold him. And as regards his baits, I have but little knowledge of them, and I would hate to write more than I know and have tested. But I know well that the earthworm and the minnow are good baits for him at all times, as I have heard reliable persons say and also found written in trustworthy books.

The chub is a stately fish, and his head is a dainty morsel. There is no fish so greatly fortified with scales on the body. And because he is a strong biter, he has the more baits, which are these. In March, the earthworm at the bottom, for usually he will bite there then, and at all times of the year if he is at all hungry. In April, the ditch canker that grows in the tree; a worm that grows between the bark and the wood of an oak; the earthworm; and the young frogs when the feet are cut off. Also, the stone fly, the grubworm under the cow turd, the red snail. In May, the bait that grows on the osier leaf and the dock canker, together upon your hook. Also a bait that grows on a fern leaf, the codworm, and a bait that grows on a hawthorn. And a bait that grows on an oak leaf and a silkworm and a codworm together. In June, take the cricket and the dor, and also an earthworm with the head cut off and a codworm in front, and put them on the hook. Also a bait on the osier leaf, young frogs with three feet cut off at the body and the fourth at the knee. The bait on the hawthorn and the codworm together; and a grub that breeds in a dunghill; and a big grasshopper. In July, the grasshopper and the bumblebee of the meadow. Also young bees and young hornets. Also a great, brindled fly that grows in paths of meadows, and the fly that is among anthills. In August, take wortworms and maggots until Michaelmas. In September, the earthworm; and also take these baits when you can get them; that is to say: cherries, young mice without hair, and the honeycomb.

The bream is a noble fish and a dainty one. And you must angle for him with an earthworm from March until August, and then with a butterfly and a green fly, and with a bait that grows among green reeds, and a bait that grows in the bark of a dead tree. And for young bream, take maggots. And from that time forth for all the year afterward, take the earthworm and, in the river, brown bread. There are more baits, but they are not easy, and therefore I pass over them.

A tench is a good fish, and heals all sorts of other fish that are hurt, if they can come to him. During most of the year he is in the mud; he stirs most in June and July, and in other seasons but little. He is a poor biter. His baits are these. For all the year, brown bread toasted with honey in the shape of a buttered loaf, and the big red worm. And for the chief bait, take the black blood in the heart of a sheep and flour and honey. Work them all together somewhat softer than paste, and anoint the earthworm therewith—both for this fish and for others. And they will bite much better thereat at all times.

The perch is a dainty fish and surpassingly wholesome, and a free-biting fish. These are his baits. In March, the earthworm. In April, the grubworm under the cow turd. In May, the sloe-thorn worm and the codworm. In June, the bait that grows in an old fallen oak, and the green canker. In July, the bait that grows on the osier leaf, and the grub that grows on the dunghill, and the hawthorn worm, and the codworm. In August, the earthworm and maggots. All the year thereafter, the earthworm is best.

The roach is an easy fish to catch. And if he is fat and penned up, then he is good food, and these are his baits. In March, the readiest bait is the earthworm. In April, the grub under the cow turd. In May, the bait that grows on the oak leaf and the grub in the dunghill. In June, the bait that grows on the osier and the codworm. In July, houseflies and the bait that grows on an oak; and the nutworm and mathewes and maggots till Michaelmas; and after that, the fat of bacon.

The dace is a noble fish to catch, and if it be well fattened, then it is good food. In March, his bait is an earthworm. In April, the grub under the cow turd. In May, the dock canker and the bait on the sloe thorn and on the oak leaf. In June, the codworm and the bait on the osier and the white grubworm in the dunghill. In July, take houseflies, and flies that grow in anthills; the codworm and maggots until Michaelmas. And if the water is clear, you will catch fish when others take none. And from that time forth, do as you do for the roach, for usually in their biting and their baits they are alike.

The bleak is but a feeble fish, yet he is wholesome. His baits from March to Michaelmas are the same as I have written before for the roach and dace, except that, all the summer season, as far as possible, you should angle for him with a housefly; and, in the winter season, with bacon and other bait made as you will know hereafter.

The ruff is a right wholesome fish, and you must angle for him with the same baits in all seasons of the year and in the same way as I have told you for the perch; for they are alike in fishing and feeding except that the ruff is smaller. And therefore he must have the smaller bait.

The flounder is a wholesome fish and a noble one, and a subtle biter in his own way. For usually, when he sucks his food, he feeds at the bottom; and therefore you must angle for him with a lying ground-line. And he has but one kind of bait, and that is an earthworm, which is the best bait for all kinds of fish.

The gudgeon is a good fish for his size, and he bites well at the bottom. And his baits for all the year are these: the earthworm, the codworm, and maggots. And you must angle for him with a float, and let your bait be near the bottom or else on the bottom.

The minnow, when he shines in the water, then he is better. And though his body is little, yet he is a ravenous biter and an eager one. And you must angle for him with the same baits as you do for gudgeon, except that they must be small.

The eel is an indigestible fish, a glutton, and a devourer of the young fry of fish. And because the pike also is a devourer of fish, I put them both behind all others for angling. For this eel, you must find a hole in the bottom of the water, and it is blue-blackish. There put in your hook till it be a foot within the hole, and your bait should be a big angle-twitch or a minnow.

The pike is a good fish, but because he devours so many of his own kind as

*well as of others, I love him the less. And to catch him, you must do thus.
Take a small cod hook, and take a roach or a fresh herring, and a wire with a
hole in the end. And put the wire in at the mouth and out at the tail, down
along the back of the fresh herring. Then put the line of your hook in after it,
and draw the hook into the cheek of the fresh herring. Then put a sinker on
your line a yard away from your hook, and a float midway between; and cast
it in a hole which the pike frequents. And this is the best and surest device for
catching the pike. There is another way of catching him. Take a frog and put it
on your hook at the back side of the neck between the skin and the body, and
put on a float a yard distant, and cast it where the pike haunts, and you will
have him. Another way: take the same bait and put it in asafetida and cast it
in the water with a cord and a cork, and you will not fail to get him. And if
you care to have good sport, then tie the cord to the foot of a goose, and you
will see a good tug-of-war to decide whether the goose or the pike will have the
better of it.*

*Now you know with what baits and how you must angle for every kind of
fish. Now I will tell you how you must keep and feed your live baits. You must
feed and keep them all together, but each kind by itself and with such things as
those in and on which they live. And as long as they are alive and fresh, they
are excellent. But when they are sloughing their skin or else dead, they are no
good. Out of these are excerpted three kinds, that is, to wit: hornets, bumblebees, and wasps. These you must bake in bread, and afterward dip their heads
in blood and let them dry. Also except maggots, which, when they are grown
large with their natural feeding, you must feed further with mutton fat and
with a cake made of flour and honey; then they will become larger. And when
you have cleansed them with sand in a bag of blanket, kept hot under your
gown or other warm thing for two or three hours, then they are best and ready
to angle with. And cut off the leg of the frog at the knee, the legs and wings of
the grasshopper at the body.*

*The following are baits made to last all the year. The first are flour and
lean meat from the hips of a rabbit or a cat, virgin wax, and sheep's fat. Bray
them in a mortar, and then mix it at the fire with a little purified honey; and
so make it up into little balls, and bait your hooks with it according to their
size. And this is a good bait for all kinds of fresh-water fish.*

*Another: take the suet of a sheep and cheese in equal amounts, and bray
them together a long time in a mortar. And then take flour and mix it
therewith, and after that mingle it with honey and make balls of it. And that
is especially for the barbel.*

*Another, for dace and roach and bleak: take wheat and seethe it well and
then put it in blood a whole day and a night, and it will be a good bait.*

For baits for great fish, keep this rule especially: When you have taken a great fish, open up the belly, and whatever you find in it, make that your bait, for it is best.

These are the twelve flies with which you must angle for the trout and grayling; and dub them just as you will now hear me tell.

March

The Dun Fly: The body of dun wool and the wings of the partridge. Another Dun Fly: the body of black wool; the wings of the blackest drake; and the jay under the wing and under the tail.

April

The Stone Fly: the body of black wool, and yellow under the wing and under the tail; and the wings, of the drake. In the beginning of May, a good fly: the body of reddened wool and lapped about with black silk; the wings, of the drake and of the red capon's hackle.

May

The Yellow Fly: the body of yellow wool; the wings of the red cock's hackle and of the drake dyed yellow. The Black Leaper: the body of black wool and lapped about with the herl of the peacock's tail; and the wings of the red capon with a blue head.

June

The Dun Cut: the body of black wool, and a yellow stripe along either side; the wings, of the buzzard, bound on with hemp that has been treated with tanbark. The Maure Fly: the body of dusky wool; the wings of the blackest breast feathers of the wild drake. The Tandy Fly at St. William's Day: the body of tandy wool; and the wings the opposite, either against the other, of the whitest breast feathers of the wild drake.

July

The Wasp Fly: the body of black wool and lapped about with yellow thread; the wings, of the buzzard. The Shell Fly at St. Thomas' Day: the body of green wool and lapped about with the herl of the peacock's tail; wings, of the buzzard.

August

The Drake Fly: the body of black wool and lapped about with black silk; wings of the breast feathers of the black drake with a black head.

These pictures are put here as examples of your hooks:

Here follows the order made to all those who shall have the understanding of this aforesaid treatise and use it for their pleasures.

You that can angle and catch fish for your pleasure, as the above treatise teaches and shows you: I charge and require you in the name of all noble men that you do not fish in any poor man's private water (such as his pond, or tank, or other things necessary for keeping fish in) without his permission and good will. And that you be not in the habit of breaking any men's fish traps lying in their weirs and in other places belonging to them, nor of taking the fish away that is caught in them. For after a fish is caught in a man's trap, if the trap is laid in the public waters, or else in such waters as he rents, it is his own personal property. And if you take it away, you are robbing him, which is a right shameful deed for any noble man to do, a thing that thieves and robbers do, who are punished for their evil deeds by the neck and otherwise when they can be discovered and captured. And also if you do in the same manner as this treatise shows you, you will have no need to take other men's fish, while you will have enough of your own catching, if you care to work for them. It will be a true pleasure to see the fair, bright, shining-scaled fishes outwitted by your crafty means and drawn out on the land. Also, I charge you, that you break no man's hedges in going about your sports, nor open any man's gates without shutting them again. Also, you must not use this aforesaid artful sport for covetousness, merely for the increasing or saving of your money, but mainly for your enjoyment and to procure the health of your body and, more especially, of your soul. For when you intend to go to your amusements in fishing, you will not want very many persons with you, who might hinder you in your pastime. And then you can serve God devoutly by earnestly saying your customary prayers. And in so doing, you will eschew and avoid many vices, such as idleness, which is the principal cause inciting a man to many other vices, as is right well known. Also, you must not be too greedy in catching your said game, as in taking too much at one time, a thing which can easily happen if you do in every point as this present treatise shows you. That could easily be the occasion of destroying your own sport and other men's also. When you have a sufficient mess, you should covet no more at that time. Also you should busy yourself to nourish the game in everything that you can, and to destroy all such things as are devourers of it. And all those that do according to this rule will have the blessing of God and St. Peter. That blessing, may He grant who bought us with his precious blood!

• • • • • •

And in order that this present treatise should not come into the hands of every idle person who would desire it if it were printed alone by itself and put in a little pamphlet, I have therefore compiled it in a larger volume of various books pertaining to gentle and noble men, to the end that the aforesaid idle persons, who would have but little moderation in the sport of fishing, should not by this means utterly destroy it.

Reprinted from *The Origins of Angling* with permission from John McDonald.